The SOURDOUGH BIBLE

3 IN 1

THE MOST COMPLETE STEP-BY-STEP GUIDE TO THE PREPARE HOMEMADE SOURDOUGH, DELICIOUS YEAST BREAD, AND PERFECT PASTRY

Lawrence M. Northern

TABLE OF CONTENTS

CHAPTER 6. SANDWICH BREADS RECIPES 110

CHAPTER 7. SWEETS RECIPES 124

INTRODUCTION

Making bread is one of the earliest human activities, and the art of doing so dates back thousands of years. Depending on local customs and ideas about what constitutes a healthy diet, people worldwide eat vast quantities of bread that taste and look very different from one another. For most of history, the only method for leavening bread was sourdough. It wasn't until the Industrial Revolution that commercial yeast was widely available, completely changing bread manufacture.

Ancient civilizations used sourdough as a kind of leavening. It is a dough made by fermenting flour and water with lactic acid bacteria and yeasts, which causes the dough to rise and creates flavor and sourness. Microflora in sourdough is initially introduced mostly via the flour, not the air, as is commonly believed. Flour already contains the "wild" yeast and bacteria needed for the sourdough fermentation process. The ingredients for a sourdough starter include flour, water, wild yeast, and lactic acid bacteria.

This starter is used in place of commercial packet yeast when preparing sourdough bread. Sourdough bread requires a longer fermenting time than store-bought alternatives. The wild yeast and bacteria degrade the gluten in the dough in the starter during fermentation, which also gives the bread its distinctive flavor and texture. This means that those who have trouble digesting gluten can eat sourdough bread.

Bread that has been fermented for a long time tastes better and keeps for a longer amount of time without the need for artificial preservatives. I'm sure you're eager to start baking sourdough bread now that you know a little bit more about sourdough starters and bread. Let's begin with the fundamentals: making a sourdough starter, feeding it, fixing problems, etc.

Whether it's traditional sourdough or Irish soda bread, there's nothing like the soft rustling of a freshly made loaf. To bake well, all you need is the patience to read a recipe through and follow the directions as written. You will be blown away by the outcome if you follow the instructions exactly.

By showing you how to recreate the basic sourdough loaf, this cookbook teaches you how to add your own spin on classic flavors with herbs, spices, cheeses, and more.

You can make fantastic sourdough at home even if you have never baked before, know nothing about food, and have only rudimentary equipment at your disposal.

Let's get started!

BOOK 1

CHAPTER 1. SOURDOUGH STARTER

What is Sourdough?

Sourdough bread is hailed as the healthiest option among the several types of bread available. In addition to being easily absorbed by the body, the vitamins and minerals found in a loaf's foundational ingredients also help to moderate the rate at which the blood absorbs glucose. This reduces the glycemic index and makes gluten in flour simpler to digest, reducing sensitivity.

Flour, water, and culture of yeast and bacteria are the main ingredients of sourdough. These microorganisms reproduce and spread at rates that are exponentially higher than those of garden weeds. Yeast cells resemble miniature bowling pins. They consume flour and release carbon dioxide as they split and multiply. The bubbles you observe in a starter are carbon dioxide gas. The bubbles, similar to the yeast in bread, prevent the pancakes or bread from becoming dense and heavy. Sourdough is referred to as "wild yeast" by certain bakers. Wild yeast and sourdough starter are interchangeable terms. It will become clear to you why sourdough has been given so many different names throughout this book. Wild yeast, sourdough, biga, and sponge are all synonymous terms that mean the same thing when they appear in a recipe. Keep this in mind while you peruse different cookbooks. In the following pages, "sourdough" will refer to sourdough starter.

To me, a sourdough starter is like a houseplant; it needs regular feeding and watering. Sourdough starters, unlike plants, can be ignored for long periods before being revived. You can keep it in the dark of the fridge for a month or put it out on the counter for a few days. Mind your step, though. Neglecting your sourdough starter can result in its demise or the introduction of dangerous molds and other bacteria that will make it unusable.

Sourdough Starter Proofing

I want to provide you with a comprehensive guide on how to proof sourdough starter. Sourdough starter is a crucial component in making sourdough bread, and the proofing process is a critical step that determines the final outcome of your bread. In this guide, I will explain the process of proofing sourdough starters in detail, so you can make perfect sourdough bread every time.

Proofing sourdough starter is the process of fermenting the mixture of flour and water to create a live, active culture that will eventually be used to make sourdough bread. Proofing, or the process of allowing the dough to rise, is a crucial step in making sourdough bread. Without proper proofing, the dough will not rise to its full potential, resulting in a dense and heavy loaf. This process involves regular feeding of the mixture with equal parts of flour and water over a period of 4-5 days until the mixture becomes active, bubbly, and has a sour, fermented aroma.

Before we begin, it's important to understand the ideal conditions for proofing sourdough starters. The temperature range should be between 70-80°F, and the location should be warm and draft-free. If your room temperature is too cold, you can place the jar in a warm place, such as a sunny windowsill or near a heat source.

Here is the recipe for making the sourdough starter.

Ingredients:

- 100g all-purpose flour
- 100g water (at room temperature)

Instructions:

1. In a clean and sterilized jar, mix 100g of all-purpose flour and 100g of water (at room temperature) until well combined and smooth, with no lumps.

2. Cover the jar with a cloth or paper towel, securing it with a rubber band. This will allow air to circulate while preventing unwanted contaminants from entering the mixture.

3. Place the jar in a warm place with a temperature range of 70-80°F for 24 hours. If the room temperature is too low, place the jar in a warm spot, such as a sunny windowsill or near a heat source.

4. Observe the mixture after 24 hours. It should have slightly expanded and have small bubbles on the surface. If not, wait another 12-24 hours and check again.

5. Once the mixture has started to ferment, discard half of it and add equal parts flour and water to the remaining mixture. For example, if you have 50g of mixture left, add 25g of flour and 25g of water. Mix well to incorporate the new flour and water.

6. Cover the jar with a cloth or paper towel, securing it with a rubber band. Leave the jar in a warm place for another 24 hours.

7. Repeat this feeding process every 24 hours for 4-5 days, discarding half of the mixture and adding equal parts flour and water. You'll notice the mixture becoming more active and bubblier with each feeding. The final mixture should have a sour, fermented aroma and have expanded significantly.

8. Your sourdough starter is ready to use in recipes or stored in the refrigerator, feeding it once a week with equal parts flour and water. To use the sourdough starter, remove the desired amount from the jar and use it in your recipe. The remaining starter can be fed as usual and stored in the refrigerator until ready to use again.

Note: The type of flour you use can affect the final flavor and texture of your sourdough starter. All-purpose flour is a good starting point, but you can experiment with other flours, such as whole wheat, rye, or spelt, to find your preferred combination.

Proofing Your Sourdough Starter:

Prepare the dough: Once you have your sourdough starter ready, you can use it to make sourdough bread. To make the dough, mix the sourdough starter with flour and water to form a sticky dough. Knead the dough on a floured surface until it becomes smooth and elastic.

Place the dough in a clean and lightly oiled bowl, cover it with a damp cloth, and let it rest for several hours or until it has doubled in size. This is known as the first rise.

Once the first rise is complete, gently punch down the dough to release the gases that have built up. Then, knead the dough briefly on a floured surface to redistribute the yeast. Divide the dough into two or more equal portions, and shape each portion into a round ball. Place the dough balls onto a lightly floured surface, cover them with a damp cloth, and let them rest for another hour or so until they have risen slightly. This is known as the second rise.

Finally, preheat your oven to 450°F (230°C), and place a cast iron Dutch oven or a heavy baking sheet in the oven to preheat as well. Once the oven is hot, and the dough has completed its second rise, carefully place the dough into the preheated Dutch oven or on the preheated baking sheet. Bake the bread for 30 to 40 minutes, or until the crust is a deep golden brown and the loaf sounds hollow when tapped. Allow the bread to cool completely on a wire rack before slicing and serving.

And that's it! With these simple steps, you can make delicious, homemade sourdough bread using your very own sourdough starter.

Sourdough Storage

This is also an important aspect for you to know and keep in mind when working with sourdough starters.

So, let's find out how to store a sourdough starter. If you feed your starter daily, once or twice a day, it will function in a very effective way.

You can keep your sourdough starter in a plastic container, in a glass jar, in a pint jar, and even in a covered pot. Our recommendation is to keep the starter in the fridge, but this is not a requirement. You can also keep it in a cold dark place in the kitchen and open it only when you need to feed it.

If you decide not to use your starter for now, you can store it by drying it. Just spread it on two pieces of parchment paper as thinly as you can using a spatula. Leave it at room temperature to completely dry (it will take a day or two), then peel it piece by piece off the parchment and keep it in a plastic bag until you need it again.

As you can see, it's pretty easy to store your sourdough for a long time. Just use our tips, and you will be able to keep your sourdough alive in the most effective and easy way.

Now that you know how to get started with sourdough, how to store it, and which tips and tricks can make this culinary experience easier, it's time to get to work and start baking.

CHAPTER 2. INGREDIENTS AND WEIGHING

There are many ways to bake, and there is no limit to making changes and additions to make delicious food in the recipes. Yet there must always be specific rules to obey to get a flawless desired outcome. You can't mix orange juice with shrimp because it tastes like feet. Similarly, there are other ranges of variations that we can make in sourdough bread to make it feel good. And for a good loaf of bread, the weight of the ingredients matters a lot. And here are the potential combinations for making delicious bread and the law for weighing the ingredients.

Types of Grains and Flour and Their Life Cycle

For the most part, wheat or rye flour prepared from whole grains is utilized whenever a new starter is created. Wild yeast is preferred over all-purpose flour in the beginning since it is less processed and has a little more food for the yeast to feed on.

Once your starter has been established, all-purpose flour can be used instead of whole-grain flour. But if you're making a whole grain loaf, you might want to use whole grain flour for the final feeding (reserving some of your initial starters to feed as usual); this will increase the amount of whole grain in the finished product and also speed up the starter slightly because of the extra yeast food in the grains.

What type of meal is best used in sourdough bread? If you're a total beginner, the best choice is organic solid white bread flour made from hard wheat. This flour will:

- Give you the fastest and highest production of gluten

- It will be the fastest to knead and shape

- It will give the best rise in the oven, but it is also useful to learn about different flours and their properties.

This knowledge will help the sourdough baker expand their baking skills and produce various types of bread.

Here's the complete information on different flours, their properties, their advantages and disadvantages, and how/why to use each in a sourdough bake.

Non-organic flour vs. Organic flour for sourdough bread:

We rely on natural organic wild-caught yeasts when it comes to sourdough bread. Therefore, it is appropriate to use organic flour to bake sourdough bread whenever possible, as it is natural and chemical-free.

Non-organic flours are also bleached, meaning that they are chemically processed to blanch the flour and age it. Organic flour has higher mineral content, so sourdough starters are better able to use flour minerals without additional chemical intervention.

What if you use non-organic flour to bake sourdough bread?

Non-organic flour gives a less flavored loaf but still provides a good rise and structure to the bread. Furthermore, it produces a more acidic and "chemically" (much like nail varnish) scented sourdough starter and a less involved sourdough starter.

Using Organic Flour

Organic flour has a slightly different mineral content profile and doesn't have the extra chemicals. So, when fermented, it provides a more authentic and nuanced flavor profile than conventional non-organic wheat flour. The truth is that a strong, mature sourdough starter still bakes wonderful bread, even if you use regular wheat instead of organic flour. If you find yourself in a tight spot financially, do not fret too much. The use of high-quality organic flour in your sourdough starter is recommended for achieving consistently great bread. However, it is possible to use whatever flour you prefer for the rest of the baking process.

Whole Wheat Flour vs. White Flour

Whatever type of wheat you choose, using whole wheat flour as opposed to a white meal can significantly alter the flavor of the bread. Whole wheat flour has a whole wheat kernel in it. This includes:

- The bran – is found on the outside of the fiber and mineral-rich wheat berry. This is the part that gives the most flavor to sourdough

- The endosperm – innermost of the wheat berry, rich in starch and mainly made up of carbohydrates and proteins. This is the part that is essential for the production of gluten in bread.

- The germ – is a small part of the vitamin-rich wheat berry. This also has left endosperm, depending on how finely it was milled.

  The use of whole wheat flour in sourdough bread adds a much more nuanced flavor profile to the final product due to the variety of minerals present in the bran.

  The bread has a denser and thicker texture. A thinner, smoother textured bread with a more open crumb (more aerated structure and larger holes) and a milder, simpler flavor profile. The whole wheat flour you have in your sourdough, the denser it gets but the more flavor it gets. This knowledge allows you to manage the bread when experimenting with different whole wheat to white flour ratios, resulting in a loaf that tastes just the way you wish it to.

Stone Ground Flour vs. Standard Flour

The use of stone-ground flour in the preparation of sourdough bread has seen a recent renaissance and shows no signs of abating. Since the advent of the industrial revolution, flour has been milled in this manner. The wheat berries are crushed between the two massive stones in this milling device. This procedure results in whole wheat flour with a higher percentage of bran. Afterward, it can be lightly sifted to remove part of the bran and transform it into white flour if desired.

The majority of flour produced now is roller milled. The process is quicker and results in finer, more uniform flour. The wheat berries are fed down the middle of two huge steel rollers, where they are smashed, and the outer bran is separated. After the bran has been removed, some of it is refined and crushed before being reintroduced to white flour to make whole wheat flour.

Stone-ground flour is ideal for a slow fermentation and results in a much more flavorful sourdough loaf. It's healthier for you since the wheat's delicate, beneficial lipids are protected from the cycle's heat and because more of the bran is preserved.

The flour's glycemic index is lower since it takes the body longer to break it down, and the flour makes for a thicker crumb thanks to the preservative characteristics of the four.

The bread made using stone-ground flour may be heavier and more difficult to slice because of the coarser texture of the flour. However, many pastry chefs insist that stoneground flour delivers "extraterrestrial" levels of flavor (and health benefits).

Use Roller Milled Flour to Make Sourdough Bread

When making sourdough bread, roller-milled flour will give you a more reliable result because of its uniform flavor, texture, and consistency. If you've never made sourdough bread before, roller-milled flour is the way to go until you figure out what works best for your particular approach.

The lack of complexity in the flavor makes this less healthy than other options. Roller milling is physically quite hard on the wheat berry, and the amount of heat created means that more nutrients are lost than in stone-ground flours.

Fine Ground vs. Coarsely Ground Flour

No matter what kind of flour you choose, the finer the flour is milled, the bigger the end product will be. It's helpful to know this in general, but it's especially relevant when considering whole wheat varieties since the ideal growing conditions for whole wheat result in a lighter loaf than those found in a single grazing soil.

Freshly milled flour, whether roller-milled or stone-ground, is in a league of its own in terms of taste, texture, and versatility.

Varieties of Wheat:

In addition to the general knowledge stated about the grain, different varieties of wheat would have different characteristics. It is important to understand these so that you can more effectively experiment with various flours and flavors. Here's a glance at some possible flours you might use for your sourdough bread and what effect they could have on the outcome of your bread.

Strong wheat: this is the most prevalent wheat type. This variety of wheat comes in a few different forms:

- Hard red winter wheat

- Hard red spring wheat

- Hard white wheat

For a beginner sourdough baker, these varieties of wheat (presuming they are white, not whole wheat) are ideal because of their high protein level. All of these wheat types reliably yield gluten of "bread quality," as the expression goes. If you use them, you won't have any trouble keeping control of them. Ancient grains fare especially well on slow fermentation by sourdough because of their many purported health benefits, such as higher nutrient density, greater digestibility, and enhanced flavor. Sourdough's already diverse flavor profile could benefit from the use of heirloom types in bread baking. What you need to know about through and its history is provided below.

Spelt flour: of the heirloom types, spelt flour is the most widely used since it is easier on the digestive system. Spelt, which has a nutty and sweet flavor, comes in both whole wheat and white variants.

Spelt has a high protein content, making it exceedingly flexible, although it is not very elastic. To put it another way, the dough can be stretched very far without returning to its original shape too quickly. The final loaf should be more compact in texture and flatter in shape but still have that delicious, somewhat spicy, nutty flavor.

You can save some water by using spelt instead of regular flour because it absorbs less liquid.

When compared to other types of wheat, einkorn flour is the most basic and easiest to digest because it is made from the first type of wheat to be farmed. It makes a gorgeous golden loaf of bread with a distinct flavor.

Distinctive features Despite being stronger in protein than other types of wheat, the composition of gluten is extremely different; excessive kneading can cause the dough to become tough. Otherwise, it will lose its flavor and turn into a gloppy mass.

Einkorn adds a crumbly, subtle texture to sourdough bread.

Ancient Egyptians used a type of wheat flour called Khorasan, sometimes known as kamut, to make bread. They still cultivate wheat for consumption in Egypt and the surrounding area. This ancient grain is packed with minerals and has a deep, satisfying taste.

Features unique to it have to do with its flexible but not elastic nature, which gives it a fluffy but very solid feel.

Because it absorbs more liquid than modern wheat, you'll need to adjust the recipe accordingly.

Rye flour: Rye flour, both light rye (sifted to extract the bran) and dark rye (whole wheat rye), and sourdough are quite close. Rye is like a super food for wild bacteria and yeasts. It is rumored to be the perfect complement to sourdough, resulting in amazing rich, fruity flavors, which is why many artisan bakeries also include rye in their sourdough bread.

Rye's unique properties include its enzyme content, which speeds up the fermentation process.

Since 100 percent rye flour with such a low strength would be too wet to knead, the best option would be to pour the dough into a loaf tin, where it would bake into a very dense but tasty loaf.

Because rye can soak up extra moisture when combined with bread flour, you may need to increase the amount of liquid in your recipe if you want to use rye. However, it can make up for the loss of density by retaining some of its moisture even after baking.

All recipes require precise flour measurements. But which measurement technique is most reliable? In this section, we will go over the three fundamental approaches of flour measurement, from the least accurate to the most exact.

While many home bakers use a scoop to measure flour, this is not an accurate method.

Why Do You Stop Scooping?

The flour is unevenly packed into the measuring cup by scooping, and each scoop will produce a different volume of the meal.

Measuring flour by volume vs. spooning

Recipes usually are written in volume. Follow the steps below to spoon in a cup of flour and take the measurements for the most precise volume calculation.

How to spoon flour:

Begin to loosen any packed areas by stirring the flour.

Using a spoon to gently scoop parts of the flour into a dry measuring cup. Do not use a cup for measuring liquid!

Fully fill out the cup allowing the flour to overfill the cup.

Use one knife's flat side or a flat spatula to place the cup over the flour canister to evenly disperse the flour into the cup. Do not push or pile down the flour because it should be free. To level the food, scrape the knife or spatula over the surface of the cup, letting the excess fall back into the flour canister.

Measuring Flour by Weight:

Weighing meals using a scale yields the most accurate results because the flour has a variable volume based on the grind, the type of grain, and the humidity.

A calibrated kitchen scale can be easily found in kitchen supplies and department stores. If you plan on baking several loaves of bread at a time, you'll want to find a scale that can weigh at least five lbs.

Additionally, keep in mind that the majority of weight-inclusive recipes are written in metric units, so picking a scale that can be adjusted to either metric or English units can save you hours of math calculations!

Beautiful baked products can be made at home for a fraction of the price of store-bought ones by precisely measuring the flour and other ingredients.

You may learn more about different sorts of meals and how they affect sourdough baking now that you are familiar with the fundamentals of measuring flour. For more tips, keep reading.

Process of Leavening

Diverse civilizations produced handmade leavening bread and other baked items before the commercial development of farmed dry and fresh baker's yeast. Sourdough is one such leavening bread that home cooks and experienced bakers make use of.

To put it simply, sourdough bread does not require additional leavening. Before industrialization, leavening bread was as easy as purchasing yeast from the shop, as evidenced by the widespread popularity of ancient Egyptian leavened bread among consumers of all ages. Sourdough bread benefits from the natural yeasts and bacteria present in the air and the flour, but "traditional" yeast baking requires adding what amounts to a concentrated dose of yeast-fungi suspended in animation to a bread dough that is otherwise extremely un-yeasty. To prevent the growth of harmful bacteria and yeasts in the dough, it is important to provide a welcoming environment for the good yeasts and bacteria that you want to encourage.

One of the essential aspects of bread making is the method of leavening using leavening agents for the bread. This reaction, in texture and flavor, is an essential part of giving bread its consistency. It's critical to comprehend how this procedure functions. In most cultures around the world, the same approach is used. It will also be served differently in some areas, such as the unleavened bread of the Middle East.

The following are several measures to help you understand the value of leavening agents for bread-like yeast and tips on how to start using leaven.

The variety of leaving agents used in baking all have properties of their own. This results in different end-product characteristics for each leavening agent employed. The taste in sourdough is not created by the yeast that is the lactobacillus (a non-spore-forming bacteria); the yeast lives with the lactobacillus in the association. The lactobacillus feeds on leftover yeast fermentation materials. It makes the part that's turning sour by lactic acid excretion. This will also stop it from spoiling anything.

Baker's yeast, a particular strain of yeast, is commonly used in bread baking. However, it is not inherently acidic due to the lack of lactobacillus and thus requires the formation of a sourdough starter. Until the 19th century, all bread loaves were sourdough because the microbial growth cycle had not yet been fully understood. When this invention was discovered by yeast scientists, bakers around the world began to adopt it. It's also important to understand the different types of grains used in bread baking.

Lactobacillus produces sourdough starter and yeast, which are similar to a mixture of pancakes. To manage a sourdough starter, extract a portion to use and add fresh flour and water to the mixture. Starters can be held for long periods, and some baking families have passed them down from generation to generation. It's also possible to buy and develop small parts of sourdough starters from specialist suppliers due to their growing ability.

A typical method for producing sourdough in families is to reserve a slice from the previous week's batch and pack the rest for the following week. If baking once a week, save a small amount of sourdough each week to grow for the following week. The starter is then mixed with new ingredients and left to rise.

Sourdough is made from a mixture of flour and yogurt dough, which takes longer to mature and ferment (8 to 14 days). It's also softer, bubblier, and sourer. It can be fed and cared for indefinitely, and some bakeries are proud of their sourdough generations.

In a recipe, sourdough is used as a leavening agent at a weight ratio of 30 percent to the total ingredients. For instance, if the flour, liquids, and other ingredients in a bread recipe exceed 1000 grams, you would need 300 grams of sourdough starter. This process takes a minimum of four hours, but it can be extended for a stronger and sourer flavor.

Different leavening agents can be used based on the desired product's shape, structure, weight, color, consistency, and preserving ability. The most relevant leavening agents are vapor, soil, biological, or chemical carbon dioxide, each recognizing different mechanisms for leavening.

The term "leavening" is often used incorrectly as a synonym for "fermentation." Instead, leavening refers to the great volume expansion of the flour. This is normally completed after frying, as the gas produced in this process is trapped in the dough's kneading.

The gas which causes leavening can be derived from: a chemical reaction between salts when using baking powder (chemical leavening), the absorption of air into the dough or water evaporation (physical leavening), or a fermentation process (biological leavening). The latter being the most common micro-organism is the yeast of the brewer (saccharomyces cerevisiae), even though micro-organisms that colonized kneading naturally were usually common. The biga had been exposed to air in the past, and only a portion of it would have been retained and used as a starter for another biga later. Natural yeast (or sourdough) consists of various microorganisms (lactic bacteria and saccharomyces), which can ferment the sugars found in the flour.

Fermentation begins with the addition of a portion of the dough from the previous knead (known as "mother dough"). The dough can be rehydrated multiple times to increase its capacity for acidification, leavening, and the number of microorganisms that aid in dough expansion. The number of refreshments and the conditions under which they can be run depends on the product that you want to get and on how much dough we need to make leavening happen.

The magic of working with the mother dough is to build and maintain a constant equilibrium between the different microbial organisms. It has been scientifically proven that it is not possible to replicate this equilibrium in vitro, but it is merely a gift from mother nature. The ability to work with sourdough lies in the ability to maintain balance over time. If the micro flora is too heterogeneous and fragile, yeasts and lactic bacteria begin a fight to win the nitrogen- and vitamin-rich fermentative substrate. The micro flora is healthy and can last over time if favorable and adequately maintained temperature and humidity conditions. The quantity and quality of the organic acids that are formed, which might change the knead rheology, as well as the ratio of the various species, are all determined by external factors. It means temperature, availability of water, oxygen, and free space by external conditions: that is, the system for preserving sourdough.

It is important to note that the method of holding sourdough, such as in a bag, water bath, or free, can have an impact on the ratio of yeasts to lactic bacteria and how the biga responds during kneading. Whether you decide to maintain your sourdough depends on the factors affecting the balance. Among them, we can find:

- The texture of sourdough
- The temperature at which sourdough is stored and fed to the starter
- The quantity of oxygen (redox potential) available in storage (anaerobiosis, oxygenation while feeding biga)
- The ratio of flour to yeasts when feeding biga.

Functional Ingredients and its Preparation

You can enjoy adding inclusions to your standard sourdough boule to mix it up and add a classic loaf to the attraction. Dried fruit, olives, beans, nuts, cheese, and herbs are some examples of inclusions.

Using baker's percentages to decide how much of the inclusion you have chosen to add to your loaf is a clear guideline.

We prefer to begin with 20 percent and adjust as necessary.

An example of this is a loaf of olives. The basic sourdough boule recipe contains 1000 grams of flour, so you can add 200 grams of olives (1000 grams x 20 percent = 200 grams) to your dough.

Now that you measure the weight of the inclusions that you add to the loaf, you are ready to start mixing.

It is recommended that you add the inclusions while doing the third fold. That is because of two main factors. First, delaying the third fold allows the dough time to strengthen its gluten without compromising the inclusions. The gluten strands may break at some additions, which could weaken them. Second, if they were added later, the dough would lose too much of its air and would not have enough time to rebound.

The following should be the order in which your dough and the ingredients are mixed:

- Mix the starter and the flour, water, and sourdough and blend until mixed. Let them remain there for 30 minutes.
- Add salt and a small quantity of water, then blend until integrated. Fold first and let sit for 30 minutes.
- Make the second fold and let it sit for 30 minutes.
- Attach the inclusions and squeeze in the dough the same way you added the salt before conducting the third fold. Do not worry if they are not distributed very evenly, as they will be mixed in even more by the next folds. Take the third fold and let it sit for 30 minutes.
- Continue as you would the simple sourdough boule with folds and rest, and form.

Baking is a consistent process, but it's important to note that if your recipe includes ingredients with high moisture content, you may need to extend the baking time. If you're unsure, it's recommended to check the internal temperature with a thermometer. The temperature should read between 190°F to 200°F.

Note: if you add an ingredient that contains a lot of moisture, it is a good idea to reduce the amount of water in your dough itself. This is going to ensure your loaf isn't square. Olives are an excellent example of extremely moisture-inducing ingredients.

Examples include:

- Cheese (cheddar, feta, parmesan)
- Dried fruit (apples, apricots, cherries, cranberries, dates, figs, peaches, pears, prunes, raisins)
- Fresh fruit (apples, apricots, cherries, cranberries, figs, peaches, pears)
- Crushed grains (barley, rye, wheat)
- Cooked rice (brown, white, wild)
- Cooked meat (bacon, ham, salami)
- Nuts (black, green, kalamata)
- Raw or toasted olives (black, green, kalamata)
- Flours (corn, spelt, teff, durum, rye)
- Liquids (water, whey, beet juice)
- Butternut squash with thyme and sauté sage
- Roasted potato and rosemary
- Rye with brotgewürz
- Oatmeal with maple syrup
- Orange zest, anise, and molasses.

Sourdough Discard

The "discard" is the clear liquid on top of the sourdough starter that you pour off when feeding to allow more room for yeast and bacteria growth. It is advisable to maintain a starter-to-water-to-flour ratio of 1:1:1, and you must discard part of the starter to control the final yield. In addition, a reduced volume of the sourdough starter means that fewer yeast cells are fighting to get enough flour "to eat."

There are three different ways of dealing with the discard:

- Throw it away anywhere far from your drain, as it often becomes cement-like after drying

- Feed the discard for a few days until it becomes active again to be used for baking
- Use it as is to make unfed sourdough and discard starter bread recipes!

Sourdough Hydration

The hydration level in baking refers to the amount of liquid or water in the dough; the more water the dough has, the higher the hydration percentage, and vice versa. The hydration levels play a big part in sourdough baking since it controls the final texture of your bread. Furthermore, it determines how the dough will react during the mixing, fermenting process, and shaping dough. Since fermentation of sough-dough bread may result in a tighter crumb, it is advisable to use the wetter dough.

For sourdough starters, keep the hydration level to around 100 percent, which means the amount of water you use should be equal to the amount of flour. However, you might prefer to keep your starter at either lower or higher concentrations for various reasons.

For instance, you may need a thicker or stiffer sourdough starter, so you'll add less amount of water for a lower hydration level. You may also need wetter dough at around 125 percent hydration level to make the starter easier to mix.

BOOK 2

CHAPTER 3. RUSTIC RECIPES

AMERICAN CHEESE BEER BREAD

Preparation time: 10 minutes

Cooking time: 60 Minutes

Servings: 8

Ingredients:

- 2 C. of fine almond flour
- 3 Tbsp. of unsalted melted butter
- 1 tsp. Salt
- 1 Large egg
- 2 Tbsp. of Swerve sweetener
- 1 C. of low-carb beer
- 1 tsp. Of baking powder
- 1 C. of cheddar cheese, shredded
- 2 tsp. of active dry yeast

Directions:

1. Preheat oven to 375°F (190°C). Grease a 9 x 5-inch loaf pan.
2. In a large mixing bowl, combine the almond flour, Swerve sweetener, salt, shredded cheddar cheese, and baking powder.
3. In a separate bowl, whisk together the melted butter, egg, and low-carb beer.
4. Add the wet ingredients to the dry ingredients and mix until just combined.
5. Add the active dry yeast and stir to combine.
6. Pour the batter into the prepared loaf pan and smooth the top.
7. Bake for 60 minutes or until a toothpick inserted into the center comes out clean.
8. Let the bread cool in the pan for 10 minutes before removing it and allowing it to cool completely on a wire rack.

Nutrition: Calories: 80, Fat: 1.5g, Carb: 13g, Protein: 3g

AMERICAN LOAF

Preparation time: 1 hour and 30 minutes

Cooking time: 1 hour

Servings: 1 loaf

Ingredients:

- 3 ½ C. white flour
- 2 tsp. salt
- 1/3 C. water
- 1 C. warm milk
- 3 tsp. honey
- 2 Tbsp. butter, melted
- 2 tsp. dry yeast
- 1 Tbsp vegetable oil

Directions:

1. In a bowl, combine the flour with the salt, water, milk, and the other ingredients, stir until you obtain a dough, knead for 10 minutes, cover the bowl, and leave aside to rise for 1 hour.
2. Shape the loaf, arrange it on a parchment paper-lined baking sheet, and leave aside to rise for 20 minutes more.
3. Bake at 350 °F for 1 hour, cool down, slice, and serve.

Nutrition/ slice: calories 100, fat 1.2, fiber 1, carbs 3.3, protein 3

BACON JALAPEÑO CHEESY BREAD

Preparation time: 5 minutes

Cooking time: 40 Minutes

Servings: 12

Ingredients:

- 1 C. golden flaxseed, ground
- 3/4 C. coconut flour
- 2 tsp. baking powder
- 1/4 tsp. black pepper
- 1 Tbsp. erythritol
- 1/3 C. pickled jalapeno
- 8 oz. cream cheese, full fat
- 4 eggs
- 3 C. sharp cheddar cheese, shredded + 1/4 cup extra for the topping
- 3 C. parmesan cheese, grated
- 1 1/4 C. almond milk
- 5 bacon slices (cooked and crumbled)
- 1/4 C. rendered bacon grease (from frying the bacon)

Directions:

1. Cook the bacon in a larger frying pan, and set aside to cool on paper towels. Save 1/4 cup of bacon fat for the recipe, and allow to cool slightly before using.
2. Add wet ingredients to the bread machine pan, including the cooled bacon grease.
3. Add in the remaining ingredients.
4. Set the quick bread setting on the bread machine.
5. When the bread is done, remove the bread machine pan from the bread machine.
6. Let it cool slightly before transferring it to a cooling rack.
7. Once on a cooling rack, top with the remaining cheddar cheese.
8. You can store your bread for up to 7 days.

Nutrition: calories 230, fat 17, fiber 4, carbs 5, protein 11

CRUSTY BREAD

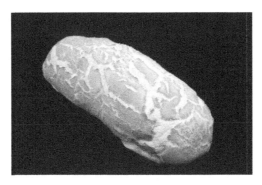

Preparation time: 2 hours and 10 minutes

Cooking time: 25 minutes

Servings: 2 loaves

Ingredients:

- 1 and ½ Tbsp. instant yeast
- 6 and ½ C. all-purpose flour
- 1 Tbsp. salt
- 3 C. warm milk
- 1 tsp. turmeric powder

Directions:

1. Take a bowl and mix the flour with the yeast and the other ingredients, stir until you obtain a dough, cover the bowl, and allow to rise for 2 hours in a warm place.
2. Shape 2 loaves, arrange them on a parchment paper lined baking sheet, and bake at 430 degrees °F for 25 minutes.
3. Cool down, slice, and serve.

Nutrition/ slice: calories 100, fat 4.3, fiber 0.6, carbs 4, protein 3.4

ETHIOPIAN BREAD

Preparation time: 10 minutes

Cooking time: 10 minutes

Servings: 6

Ingredients:

- 2 C. white flour
- Juice of 2 limes
- 1 tsp. salt
- 2 C. sparkling water
- 1 Tbsp. baking powder
- Cooking spray

Directions:

1. In a bowl, combine the flour with salt, water, baking powder, and lime juice and stir well.
2. Grease a pan with cooking spray, heat up over medium heat, pour ½ cup of the bread batter you've made, spread, and cook for 2 about minutes on each side.
3. Repeat with the remaining batter, cool the bread down, roll, and serve them.

Nutrition/ roll: calories 89, fat 0.5, fiber 0, carbs 1, protein 1.1

GOAT CHEESE CRACKERS

Preparation Time: 5 minutes

Cooking Time: 20 minutes

Servings: 12

Ingredients:

- 6 oz. goat cheese
- ½ C. coconut flour
- 4 Tbsp. butter
- 2 Tbsp. fresh rosemary
- 1 tsp. baking powder

Directions:

1. In a food processor, combine all ingredients and mix until smooth.
2. Roll out the dough with a rolling pin to about ¼ to ½ inch thick and cut out the crackers with a knife or cookie cutter.
3. Line a baking sheet using parchment paper and place the crackers on it.
4. Bake at 380°F for 15 to 20 minutes.

Nutrition/cracker: calories 99, fat 8, fiber 1, carbs 2, protein 4

INDIAN BREAD

Preparation time: 1 hour and 30 minutes

Cooking time: 10 minutes

Servings: 12

Ingredients:

- 4 Tbsp. sugar
- 2 tsp. salt
- 4 C. white flour
- 1 tsp dry yeast
- 1 C. warm milk
- 1 egg, whisked
- 4 Tbsp. butter, melted

Directions:

1. In a large bowl, mix the sugar with salt, flour, and yeast and stir.
2. Add the rest of the ingredients, knead the mix until you obtain an elastic dough, cover the bowl, and allow it to rise for 1 hour.
3. Divide the dough into 12 balls and allow them to rise for 30 minutes more.
4. Heat up your grill over medium-high heat, flatten the balls, cook them for 4 minutes one each side, and serve.

Nutrition/ bread: calories 76, fat 1.2, fiber 0.8, carbs 1, protein 1.2

ITALIAN BLUE CHEESE BREAD

Preparation time: 3 hours

Cooking Time: 30 minutes

Servings: 8

Ingredients:

- 1 tsp. dry yeast
- 2 ½ C. almond flour
- 1 ½ tsp. salt
- 1 Tbsp. sugar
- 1 Tbsp. olive oil
- ½ C. blue cheese
- 1 C. of water

Directions

1. In a large bowl, dissolve the yeast in warm water and let it stand for 5-10 minutes until the yeast is frothy.
2. Add the almond flour, salt, sugar, and olive oil to the yeast mixture and stir until a dough forms.
3. Add the crumbled blue cheese to the dough and knead until well incorporated.
4. Place the dough in a greased bowl, cover it, and let it rise in a warm place for 2 hours.
5. Preheat the oven to 450°F.
6. Punch down the dough and form it into a loaf. Place the loaf in a greased baking pan.
7. Bake for 30 minutes or until the loaf is golden brown and sounds hollow when tapped.
8. Let the bread cool on a wire rack before slicing and serving.

Nutrition: calories 194, fat 7, fiber 4, carbs 12, protein 6

MEXICAN RUSTIC LOAF

Preparation time: 2 hours and 10 minutes

Cooking time: 20 minutes

Servings: 2 loaves

Ingredients:

- 4 C. white flour
- 2/3 C. sugar
- 1 C. milk
- ½ C. butter
- 2 tsp. dry yeast
- 1 tsp. cinnamon powder
- 1 egg
- 1 tsp. vanilla extract

Directions:

1. In a large bowl, mix the flour with the sugar, milk, and the other ingredients, stir until you obtain a dough, cover, and leave aside for 2 hours.
2. Shape the loaves, place them on a parchment paper lined baking sheet, and bake at 435°F for 20 minutes.
3. Cool down, slice, and serve.

Nutrition/ slice: calories 121, fat 1.2, fiber 2.3, carbs 0.3, protein 1.1

PARMESAN ITALIAN BREAD

Preparation Time: 45 minutes

Cooking Time: 30 minutes

Servings: 10

Ingredients:

- 1 1/3 C. warm water
- 2 Tbsp. olive oil
- 2 cloves of garlic, crushed
- 1 Tbsp. basil
- 1 Tbsp. oregano
- 1 Tbsp. parsley
- 2 C. almond flour
- 1 Tbsp. inulin
- 1/2 C. parmesan cheese, grated
- 1 tsp. active dry yeast

Directions:

1. In a large bowl, combine the warm water, olive oil, crushed garlic, and yeast. Stir until the yeast is dissolved.
2. Add the basil, oregano, parsley, almond flour, inulin, and parmesan cheese to the bowl. Mix well until the dough forms.
3. Turn the dough onto a floured surface and knead for about 5-10 minutes until smooth.
4. Place the dough into a greased bowl, cover it with a clean cloth, and let rise in a warm place for 30-40 minutes or until doubled in size.
5. Preheat your oven to 425°F. Grease a 9x5-inch loaf pan.
6. Once the dough has risen, punch it down and shape it into a loaf. Place the dough into the prepared loaf pan.
7. Bake in the preheated oven for 30-35 minutes or until the loaf is golden brown and sounds hollow when tapped on the bottom.
8. Remove the bread from the oven and transfer it to a wire rack to cool completely.
9. Enjoy your delicious parmesan Italian bread!

Nutrition: calories 150, fat 7, fiber 4, carbs 12, protein 5

RICOTTA BREAD

Preparation Time: 3 hours

Cooking Time: 30 minutes

Servings: 10

Ingredients:

- 1/3 C. milk
- 1 C. ricotta cheese
- 2 Tbsp. butter
- 1 egg
- 2 ½ Tbsp. sugar
- 1 tsp. salt
- 2 ¼ C. bread flour
- 1 ½ tsp. yeast

Directions:

1. Put all of the bread ingredients in your bread machine in the order listed above, starting with the milk and finishing with the yeast.

2. Make a well in the middle of the flour and place the yeast in the well. Make sure the well doesn't touch any liquid. Set the bread machine to the basic function with a light crust.

3. Check on the dough after about 5 minutes, and make sure that it's a soft ball. Add water one tablespoon at a time if it's too dry, and add flour one tablespoon at a time if it's too wet.

4. When the bread is done, allow it to cool on a wire rack.

Nutrition: calories 115, fat 6, fiber 1, carbs 3, protein 9

RUSTIC HONEY BREAD

Preparation time: 5 hours and 10 minutes

Cooking time: 40 minutes

Servings: 1 loaf

Ingredients:

- 3 C. all-purpose flour
- ¾ C. active sourdough starter
- 1 ¼ C. warm water
- 1 Tbsp. honey
- 1 ½ tsp. salt

Directions:

1. In a large bowl, mix the flour with the other ingredients, stir well until you obtain a dough, cover the bowl, and let the dough rise for 5 hours.
2. Transfer to a loaf pan and bake at 450 degrees °F for 40 minutes.
3. Leave the loaf to cool down, slice, and serve.

Nutrition/ slice: calories 119, fat 0.2, fiber 0.8, carbs 24, protein 3.2

RUSTIC SOURDOUGH BREAD

Preparation time: 2 hours and 40 minutes

Cooking time: 30 minutes

Servings: 2 loaves

Ingredients:

- 1 C. mature sourdough starter
- 2 C. warm water
- 4 tsp. salt
- 7 to 8 C. bread flour or all-purpose flour

Directions:

1. In a large bowl, mix the mature sourdough starter with the water and 4 cups of flour. Stir until a rough dough forms, then cover and let it sit for about 4 hours.

2. Add the salt and gradually add more flour until the dough is no longer sticky and forms a cohesive ball. Knead the dough for several minutes, then cover it and let it rise for about 12 to 16 hours.

3. Divide the dough in half and shape it into two round loaves. Place the loaves on a piece of parchment paper, cover and let them rise for another 2 to 4 hours.

4. Preheat your oven to 450°F (230°C) with a Dutch oven or heavy baking sheet inside. When the oven is fully heated, carefully place the risen loaves in the pot or on the sheet, and score the tops of the loaves with a sharp knife or razor blade.

5. Bake for 30 minutes or until the crust is golden brown and the loaves sound hollow when tapped. Let the loaves cool completely on a wire rack before slicing and serving.

Nutrition/ slice: calories 80, fat 0, fiber 1, carbs 17, protein 5

SPICED RUSTIC BREAD

Preparation time: 1 hour and 10 minutes

Cooking time: 1 hour

Servings: 1 loaf

Ingredients:

- 1 egg, whisked
- ½ C. honey
- ¼ C. warm water
- 4 C. white flour
- 1 tsp. coriander, ground
- 1 tsp. ginger, ground
- 1 tsp. cloves, ground
- 1 tsp. cinnamon powder
- 2 tsp. salt
- 3 Tbsp. butter, melted

Directions:

1. In a bowl, mix the flour with coriander and the other dry ingredients and stir.
2. In a separate large bowl, mix the egg with the wet ingredients and stir again.
3. Combine the 2 mixtures and start kneading until you obtain an elastic dough; cover the bowl and leave aside for 1 hour.
4. Shape your loaf, arrange it on a lined baking sheet, and bake at 300 F for 1 hour.
5. Cool down, slice, and serve.

Nutrition/ slice: calories 80, fat 2, fiber 0.7, carbs 1.1, protein 0.8

SUGAR-FREE CREAM CHEESE FROSTING

Preparation Time: 5 minutes

Cooking Time: nil

Servings: 6

Ingredients:

- 4oz cream cheese
- 2 Tbsp. butter, cubed, softened
- 1/2 C. erythritol, powder or granulated
- 1 tsp. vanilla extract
- 1 Tbsp. heavy cream

Directions:

1. In a mixing bowl, combine the cream cheese, butter, erythritol, and vanilla extract.

2. Using a hand mixer, beat the ingredients until smooth and well combined.

3. Slowly add in 1 tablespoon of heavy cream at a time, and continue beating until the desired consistency is reached. If the frosting is too thick, add in more heavy cream, 1 tablespoon at a time, until it reaches the desired consistency.

4. Use the frosting immediately or store it in the refrigerator for up to 5 days.

Nutrition: calories 12, fat 7, fiber 4, carbs 9, protein 2

SODA BREAD

Preparation Time: 10 minutes

Cooking Time: 1.5 hours

Serving: 8

Dry Ingredients:

- 2 C. almond flour
- ½ C. coconut flour
- ½ C. no-calorie sweetener of your choice
- ¼ C. raisins, chopped
- 3 Tbsp. butter, softened
- 2 tsp. baking powder
- ½ tsp. baking soda
- ¼ tsp. salt

Wet Ingredients:

- 2 eggs
- 1 C. buttermilk

Directions:

1. Add the ingredients to the bread pan in the following order: buttermilk, eggs, sweetener, salt, baking soda, baking powder, flour, butter, and raisins.
2. Use the "Quick" or "Cake" setting of the bread machine.
3. Wait until all cycles are finished.
4. Remove the pan from the machine.
5. Wait for another 10 minutes before taking out the bread from the pan.
6. Slice only when the bread has completely cooled down.

Nutrition: calories 110, fat 6, fiber 4, carbs 6, protein 4

RUSTIC GERMAN BREAD

Preparation time: 5 hours

Cooking time: 45 minutes

Servings: 1 big loaf

Ingredients:

- 3 C. all-purpose flour
- 1 ½ C. warm water
- 1 tsp. active dry yeast
- 3 Tbsp. honey
- 2 Tbsp. caraway seeds
- 2 tsp. salt
- 2 Tbsp. olive oil

Directions:

1. In a large bowl, mix together the flour, yeast, honey, caraway seeds, salt, and olive oil. Gradually add in the warm water, stirring until a dough forms.

2. Turn the dough out onto a lightly floured surface and knead for about 10 minutes until smooth and elastic.

3. Place the dough back into the bowl, cover it with plastic wrap, and let it rise in a warm place for about 2 hours or until doubled in size.

4. Preheat your oven to 425°F. Line a baking sheet with parchment paper.

5. Turn the dough out onto a lightly floured surface and shape it into a large round loaf. Place the loaf on the prepared baking sheet.

6. Bake for about 45 minutes, or until the bread is golden brown and sounds hollow when tapped on the bottom.

7. Allow the bread to cool completely on a wire rack before slicing and serving.

Nutrition/ slice: calories 99, fat 1.2, fiber 2.1, carbs 1.4, protein 2

PITA BREAD

Preparation time: 3 hours

Cooking time: 10 minutes

Servings: 8

Ingredients:

- 2 C. white flour
- 1 C. warm water
- 1 tsp. salt
- ½ tsp. black pepper
- 1 tsp. dry yeast
- 2 ½ Tbsp. olive oil

Directions:

1. In a bowl, mix the flour with water, salt, pepper, yeast, and ½ tablespoon oil; knead until you obtain an elastic dough, cover the bowl, and leave aside to rise for 2 hours.
2. Divide the dough into 8 balls, cover the bowl again, and leave aside to rise for 1 more hour.
3. Heat up a pan with the remaining oil over medium-high heat, flatten a ball into a circle, place it in the pan, and cook for 5 minutes on each side.
4. Repeat with the rest of the dough balls and serve.

Nutrition/ pita: calories 45, fat 0.1, fiber 1, carbs 0.7, protein 0.6

IRISH TASTY LOAF

Preparation time: 1 hour and 10 minutes

Cooking time: 50 minutes

Serving: 1 loaf

Ingredients:

- 4 Tbsp. sugar
- ½ C. margarine
- 1 C. buttermilk
- 4 C. white flour
- 1 tsp. salt
- 1 tsp. baking soda
- 1 egg, whisked

Directions:

1. In a large bowl, mix the sugar with the flour, salt, and baking soda, stir, and leave aside for 10 minutes.
2. Add the rest of the ingredients and stir until you obtain a dough; cover the bowl and leave aside to rise for 1 hour.
3. Transfer to a loaf pan, introduce in the oven, and bake at 375 degrees °F for 50 minutes.
4. Cool the loaf dough, slice, and serve.

Nutrition/ slice: calories 99, fat 1.1, fiber 0.8, carbs 1.9, protein 0.6

ISRAELI LOAF

Preparation time: 3 hours and 30 minutes

Cooking time: 40 minutes

Servings: 3 loaves

Ingredients:

- 8 C. white flour
- 1 tsp. poppy seeds
- 2 ½ C. warm water
- 1 Tbsp. dry yeast
- 4 Tbsp. vegetable oil
- 3 eggs, whisked

Directions:

1. In a large bowl, mix the flour with yeast and poppy seeds and stir.
2. Add the rest of the ingredients, stir well, knead the dough for 15 minutes, cover the bowls, and leave aside to rise for 3 hours.
3. Divide the dough into 3 loaf pans and leave them aside to rise for 15 more minutes.
4. Bake at 400 degrees °F for 40 minutes, cool down, and serve.

Nutrition/ slice: calories 101, fat 1.2, fiber 0, carbs 1.6, protein 1.1

RUSSIAN BREAD

Preparation time: 3 hours and 10 minutes

Cooking time: 40 minutes

Servings: 2 loaves

Ingredients:

- 3 C. white flour
- 2 C. warm water
- 2 Tbsp. cider vinegar
- ½ tsp. coriander, ground
- 1 Tbsp. brown sugar
- 1 Tbsp. coffee
- 1 tsp. salt
- 1 tsp. fennel seeds, crushed
- 2 Tbsp. corn syrup
- 2 tsp. dry yeast
- 3 Tbsp. butter, melted

Directions:

1. In a large bowl, mix the flour with coriander, sugar, coffee, salt, fennel, and yeast, and stir well.
2. In a separate bowl, mix the water with the rest of the ingredients, stir as well, and leave aside for 10 minutes.
3. Combine the 2 mixtures, stir until you obtain a dough, knead, cover, and leave aside for 2 hours.
4. Shape the 2 loaves, divide them in loaf pans, and leave them aside to rise for 1 more hour.
5. Bake at 400 degrees for 40 minutes and serve completely cold.

Nutrition/ slice: calories 110, fat 1.4, fiber 1, carbs 2, protein 2.2

FRENCH LOAF

Preparation time: 2 hours and 10 minutes

Cooking time: 45 minutes

Servings: 2 loaves

Ingredients:

- 1 Tbsp. yeast
- 2 C. warm water
- 1 Tbsp. vegetable oil
- 1 tsp. nutmeg, ground
- 1 tsp. cumin, ground
- 1 tsp. ginger, ground
- 5 C. white flour
- 1 Tbsp. sugar

Directions:

1. Take a bowl and mix the flour with the cumin, nutmeg, ginger, sugar, and yeast and stir well.
2. Add the rest of the ingredients, stir and knead the dough, cover, and leave aside in a warm place for 2 hours.
3. Transfer the dough to 2 loaf pans and bake at 400 degrees °F for 45 minutes.
4. Cool the loaf down, slice, and serve.

Nutrition/ slice: calories 99, fat 1.2, fiber 1, carbs 2.1, protein 0.9

CRISPY HUNGARIAN BREAD

Preparation time: 3 hours and 30 minutes

Cooking time: 50 minutes

Servings: 1 loaf

Ingredients:

- 2 tsp. dry yeast
- 4 C. bread flour
- 1 tsp. salt
- 1 ½ C. warm almond milk
- 1 egg yolk, beaten
- 1 Tbsp. cumin, ground
- 1 Tbsp. sugar
- 1 Tbsp. vegetable oil

Directions:

1. In a bowl, mix the flour with salt, cumin, sugar, and yeast and stir well.
2. Add the rest of the ingredients, knead for 15 minutes, cover the bowl, and leave aside for 3 hours.
3. Transfer to a loaf pan, leave the pan aside for 30 minutes more, and bake at 390 degrees °F for 50 minutes.
4. Cool the loaf down, slice, and serve.

Nutrition/ slice: calories 110, fat 1.2, fiber 2, carbs 1.2, protein 2.1

HERBED LOAF

Preparation time: 2 hours and 10 minutes

Cooking time: 1 hour

Servings: 1 loaf

Ingredients:

- 2 tsp. dry yeast
- 1 C. warm milk
- 2 Tbsp. butter, melted
- 3 Tbsp. honey
- 3 C. white flour (bread or all-purpose)
- 1 tsp. salt
- 2/3 C. chives, chopped
- ½ tsp. black pepper

Directions:

1. In a bowl, mix the flour with the yeast, salt, pepper, and chives and stir.
2. Add the rest of the ingredients, knead the dough for 15 minutes, cover the bowls, and leave aside to rise for 2 hours.
3. Transfer to a loaf pan, bake at 380 degrees °F for 1 hour, cool down, slice, and serve.

Nutrition/slice: calories 88, fat 0.2, fiber 1.1, carbs 1.2, protein 1

SIMPLE BAGUETTE

Preparation time: 2 hours
Cooking time: 40 minutes
Servings: 3 baguettes

Ingredients:

- 1 C. white flour
- ¼ C. psyllium husk
- 2 Tbsp. baking soda
- ¼ C. corn starch
- 1 tsp. salt
- 1 egg, whisked
- 1 tsp. turmeric powder
- 1 ½ C. warm water
- 1 tsp. dry yeast
- 1 Tbsp. baking fibers

Directions:

1. In a bowl, mix the flour with the baking soda, cornstarch, and the other ingredients except for the egg and the water and stir.
2. Add the egg and stir the mix again.
3. Add the water gradually and stir until you obtain a dough.
4. Cover the bowl with the dough and leave aside in a warm place for 2 hours.
5. Shape 3 logs out of this dough, arrange them on a lined baking sheet, leave them 10 more minutes to rise, and then bake them at 400 degrees °F for 40 minutes.
6. Cool the baguettes down and serve.

Nutrition/ baguette: calories 242, fat 2.8, fiber 2.3, carbs 4, protein 1.2

SPICY RUSTIC BREAD

Preparation time: 2 hours and 10 minutes

Cooking time: 50 minutes

Servings: 2 loaves

Ingredients:

- ¼ C. sriracha sauce
- ½ C. warm water
- 1 egg, whisked
- 3 C. white flour
- 1 Tbsp. vegetable oil
- 1 tsp. salt
- 1 tsp. butter, melted

Directions:

1. In a bowl, mix the flour with the salt and the other ingredients and stir well until you obtain a dough.
2. Move the dough to a working surface and knead for 10 minutes.
3. Return the dough to a bowl, cover, and rise for 2 hours.
4. Divide the dough into 2 loaf pans and bake at 390 degrees °F for 50 minutes.
5. Cool the bread down, slice, and serve.

Nutrition/ slice: calories 88, fat 2.2, fiber 2.0, carbs 1.8, protein 2

RUSTIC CHEESE BREAD

Preparation time: 1 hour and 30 minutes

Cooking time: 40 minutes

Servings: 2 loaves

Ingredients:

- 2 tsp. baking powder
- 2 C. white flour
- 1 tsp. salt
- ¼ C. sugar
- 1 C. almond milk
- 3 Tbsp. vegetable oil
- 1 C. cheddar cheese, grated

Directions:

1. In a bowl, mix the flour with the salt, baking powder, and the other ingredients, stir, knead the dough, cover the bowl, and allow it to rise for 1 hour.
2. Divide the dough into 2 loaf pans and allow them to rise for 30 minutes more.
3. Bake the bread at 420 degrees °F for 40 minutes.

Nutrition/ slice: calories 111, fat 2.1, fiber 2, carbs 1.1, protein 2.2

POTATO BREAD

Preparation time: 2 hours and 10 minutes

Cooking time: 50 minutes

Servings: 2 loaves

Ingredients:

- 1 ½ C. warm water
- 2 Tbsp. shortening
- 2 Tbsp. sugar
- 2 tsp. dry yeast
- 1 potato, baked, peeled, and grated
- 4 C. bread flour
- 1 tsp. salt

Directions:

1. In a bowl, mix the water with the shortening, sugar, and the other ingredients, stir, knead well, cover the bowl, and leave aside to rise for 2 hours.
2. Divide the dough into 2 loaves, leave them to rise for 10 more minutes, and bake at 395 degrees °F for 50 minutes.
3. Cool down, slice, and serve.

Nutrition/ slice: calories 111, fat 2.2, fiber 0.8, carbs 1.8, protein 2.2

CHAPTER 4. WHOLE GRAIN BREAD RECIPES

AVOCADO WHOLE WHEAT BREAD

Preparation time: 10 minutes

Cooking time: 40 minutes

Servings: 1 loaf

Ingredients:

- 1 C. whole wheat flour
- 1 tsp. baking powder
- 1 tsp. cinnamon powder
- ½ C. sugar
- 1 egg, whisked
- 4 Tbsp. butter, melted
- ½ tsp. vanilla extract
- 1 tsp. lemon juice
- 1 C. avocado, peeled, pitted, and mashed

Directions:

1. In a bowl, mix the flour with baking powder, cinnamon, and the other ingredients and stir well until you obtain a dough.
2. Knead the dough for 10 minutes, transfer to a loaf pan, and bake it at 320 degrees °F for 40 minutes.
3. Cool the bread down, slice, and serve.

Nutrition/ loaf: calories 254, fat 6.5, fiber 3.4, carbs 6.5, protein 6

BROCCOLI RYE BREAD

Preparation Time: 10 minutes

Cooking Time: 40 minutes

Servings: 1 loaf

Ingredients:

- 1 C. broccoli, grated
- 1 C. cheddar cheese, shredded
- 1 C. rye flour
- 1 C. all-purpose flour
- 5 eggs, whisked
- 2 tsp. baking powder
- 1 tsp. salt
- 1 Tbsp. olive oil or melted butter
- Cooking spray

Directions

1. Preheat the oven to 350 degrees F (180 degrees C). Grease a 9x5-inch loaf pan with cooking spray.
2. In a large bowl, mix the grated broccoli and cheese together.
3. In a separate bowl, whisk together the flour, baking powder, and salt.
4. Add the flour mixture to the broccoli mixture and stir until well combined.
5. Stir in the eggs and olive oil or melted butter until a dough forms.
6. Knead the dough for about 2 minutes and then shape it into a loaf.
7. Place the loaf in the prepared loaf pan and bake for 40 minutes or until a toothpick inserted into the center comes out clean.
8. Allow the bread to cool in the pan for 10 minutes, then transfer it to a wire rack to cool completely.
9. Slice the bread and serve.

Nutrition/ loaf: calories 273, fat 7.6, fiber 3.4, carbs 4.4, protein 5.4

BUTTER WHOLE WHEAT BUNS

Preparation Time: 10 minutes

Cooking Time: 12 minutes

Servings: 4 buns

Ingredients:

- 1 C. whole wheat flour
- 1 Tbsp. sugar
- 2 tsp. baking powder
- 1/2 tsp. salt
- 2 Tbsp. unsalted butter, melted
- 1/4 C. milk
- 1 large egg
- 2 Tbsp. psyllium husk
- Cooking spray

Directions:

1. Preheat the oven to 375°F (190°C). Line a baking sheet with parchment paper or a silicone mat and lightly spray with cooking spray.

2. In a large bowl, whisk together the whole wheat flour, sugar, baking powder, and salt.

3. In a separate bowl, whisk together the melted butter, milk, egg, and psyllium husk.

4. Pour the wet ingredients into the dry ingredients and stir until a soft dough forms.

5. Divide the dough into 4 equal portions and shape each into a ball. Place the buns on the prepared baking sheet, leaving about 2 inches between each.

6. Bake the buns for 18-20 minutes, or until they are lightly golden and a toothpick inserted into the center comes out clean.

7. Allow the buns to cool on the baking sheet for a few minutes before serving.

Nutrition/bun: calories 142, fat 4.3, fiber 3.4, carbs 6.5, protein 2.3

CHILI QUINOA LOAF

Preparation Time: 10 minutes

Cooking Time: 25 minutes

Servings: 1 loaf

Ingredients:

- 1 and ½ C. quinoa, cooked
- ½ C. all-purpose flour
- ½ C. flaxseed meal
- 2 eggs, whisked
- 1 tsp. baking powder
- 1 tsp. baking soda
- 1 tsp. salt
- ½ C. sour cream
- 3 Tbsp. butter, soft
- 1 Tbsp. sugar
- 2 red chili peppers, minced
- ½ C. cheddar cheese, grated
- Cooking spray

Directions:

1. Preheat the oven to 375°F (190°C). Grease a 9x5-inch loaf pan with cooking spray and set aside.
2. In a large bowl, cream the butter and sugar together until light and fluffy.
3. Add the quinoa, flour, flaxseed meal, eggs, baking powder, baking soda, salt, sour cream, chili peppers, and cheese to the bowl. Stir until well combined.
4. Transfer the dough to the prepared loaf pan and bake for 25 minutes or until a toothpick inserted in the center comes out clean.
5. Cool the loaf in the pan for 5 minutes, then transfer it to a wire rack to cool completely.
6. Slice and serve. Enjoy!

Nutrition/ loaf: calories 200, fat 12.2, fiber 3.4, carbs 8.5, protein 5.3

COCONUT CORN BREAD

Preparation Time: 10 minutes

Cooking Time: 50 minutes

Servings: 1 loaf

Ingredients:

- ½ C. coconut flour
- ½ C. corn flour
- 1 tsp. oregano, dried
- 1 tsp. basil, dried
- 5 eggs, whisked
- 6 Tbsp. butter, melted
- 1 tsp. baking soda
- 1 tsp. garlic powder
- ½ tsp. black pepper
- ½ tsp. salt

Directions:

1. In a large bowl, mix the flour with oregano, basil, and the other ingredients, stir until you obtain a dough, knead it for 10 minutes, and transfer to a loaf pan lined with parchment paper.
2. Bake at 340 degrees °F for 50 minutes, cool down, slice, and serve.

Nutrition/ loaf: calories 172, fat 4.3, fiber 2.3, carbs 4.4, protein 6

CORN SHORTBREAD

Preparation Time: 30 minutes

Cooking Time: 15 minutes

Servings: 8

Ingredients:

- 2 C. corn flour
- 5 Tbsp. ghee, melt
- 1 Tbsp. lemon zest, grated
- 4 Tbsp. sugar
- 1 Tbsp. lemon juice
- 1 tsp. vanilla extract
- 1 tsp. baking powder
- 1 tsp. rosemary, dried

Directions:

1. In a bowl, mix the flour with the lemon zest, sugar, baking powder, and rosemary and stir.
2. Add the other ingredients gradually, stir well until you obtain a dough, make a log, wrap it in plastic, and keep it in the freezer for 30 minutes.
3. Cut the log into circles, arrange it on a baking sheet lined with parchment paper, and cook at 370 degrees °F for 15 minutes before cooling down and serving.

Nutrition/ piece: calories 100, fat 2.3, fiber 2.3, carbs 3.4, protein 4.3

DUTCH OVEN SPELT BREAD

Preparation Time: 30 minutes

Cooking Time: 40 minutes

Servings: 1 loaf

Ingredients:

- 1 ½ C. almond flour
- 1 ½ C. spelt flour
- 1 tsp. baking powder
- 1 tsp. baking soda
- ½ tsp. salt
- 1 tsp. sugar
- 1 ½ C. warm water

Directions:

1. In a bowl, mix the flour with baking powder, soda, and the other ingredients, stir, and knead until you obtain a dough.
2. Cover the bowl and leave the dough to rise for 30 minutes.
3. Transfer to a Dutch oven, bake at 400 degrees °F for 40 minutes, cool down, slice, and serve.

Nutrition/ loaf: calories 242, fat 6.5, fiber 3.3, carbs 6.4, protein 4.3

FLAX BREAD

Preparation Time: 10 minutes

Cooking Time: 45 minutes

Servings: 1 bread

Ingredients:

- 1 C. flaxseed meal
- 4 eggs, whisked
- 1 C. coconut flour
- 1 tsp. baking powder
- 1 tsp. baking soda
- 1 tsp. salt
- 1 Tbsp. apple cider vinegar
- ½ C. warm water

Directions:

1. In a bowl, mix the coconut flour with a flaxseed meal and the other ingredients except for the eggs and the water and stir.
2. Add the water and eggs, stir, and knead until you obtain a dough.
3. Transfer it to a loaf pan and bake at 350 degrees °F for 40 minutes before cooling and serving.

Nutrition/ loaf: calories 300, fat 12, fiber 1.2, carbs 4.3, protein 9.2

FLAX STEVIA BREAD

Preparation Time: 10 minutes

Cooking Time: 45 minutes

Servings: 1 loaf

Ingredients:

- 2 Tsp. baking powder
- 1 ½ C. protein isolate
- 1 tsp. salt
- 2 C. flax seed meal
- 4 egg whites, whisked
- 1 whole egg, whisked
- 1 C. water
- ¼ C. stevia
- 2 Tbsp. coconut oil, melted

Directions:

1. Preheat oven to 350°F (175°C).
2. In a large mixing bowl, combine the flaxseed meal, protein isolate, baking powder, salt, and stevia.
3. In a separate mixing bowl, whisk together the egg whites, whole egg, water, and melted coconut oil.
4. Add the wet ingredients to the dry ingredients and stir until well combined.
5. Pour the batter into a 9x5-inch loaf pan that has been greased or lined with parchment paper.
6. Bake for 45 minutes or until a toothpick inserted into the center of the loaf comes out clean.
7. Allow the loaf to cool for 10 minutes before slicing and serving.

Nutrition/ slice: calories 87, fat 1.2, fiber 0.7, carbs 3, protein 2.2

MOZZARELLA RYE BAGELS

Preparation Time: 10 minutes

Cooking Time: 20 minutes

Servings: 4

Ingredients:

- 1 C. rye flour
- 1 C. mozzarella, shredded
- 1 Tbsp. cream cheese
- 1 tsp. salt
- 1 egg, whisked
- 1 Tbsp. sesame seeds
- 1 Tbsp. butter, melted
- 1 tsp. sugar

Directions:

1. In a bowl, mix the flour with mozzarella and the other ingredients except the sesame seeds and butter and stir until you obtain a firm dough.
2. Divide into 4 pieces and divide them into donut pans.
3. Brush them with the butter, sprinkle them with sesame seeds, and cook at 380 degrees °F for 20 minutes.

Nutrition/ bagel: calories 200, fat 4.3, fiber 2.3, carbs 5.4, protein 7.6

NUTMEG ASPARAGUS BREAD

Preparation Time: 10 minutes

Cooking Time: 45 minutes

Servings: 1 loaf

Ingredients:

- 1 C. sugar
- 1 C. avocado oil
- 2 C. corn flour
- 2 egg whites, whisked
- 1 tsp. baking powder
- 1 tsp. nutmeg, ground
- ½ tsp. salt
- Cooking spray
- 2 C. asparagus, steamed and chopped

Directions:

1. In a large bowl, mix the flour with the sugar, oil, and the other ingredients except for the cooking spray, stir well until you obtain a dough, cover the bowl, and leave aside for 10 minutes.
2. Transfer the dough to a loaf pan greased with cooking spray and bake at 350 degrees °F for 45 minutes.
3. Cool the bread down, slice, and serve.

Nutrition/ loaf: calories 200, fat 3.4, fiber 3.3, carbs 8.7, protein 3.4

PARMESAN RICE BREAD

Preparation Time: 1 hour and 10 minutes

Cooking Time: 40 minutes

Servings: 2 loaves

Ingredients:

- 1 C. parmesan, grated
- 1 C. rice flour
- 1 ½ C. warm water
- 1 tsp. instant yeast
- 1 tsp. baking powder
- 1 tsp. salt
- 1 tsp. black pepper
- 1 garlic clove, minced

Directions:

1. In a large bowl, mix the flour with the water and the other ingredients, stir until you obtain a dough, cover the bowl, and leave aside for 1 hour.
2. Divide the dough into 2 loaf pans, bake the bread at 390 degrees °F for 40 minutes, cool down, slice, and serve.

Nutrition/ loaf: calories 272, fat 5.4, fiber 2.4, carbs 5.4, protein 3.4

RYE PUMPKIN BREAD

Preparation Time: 10 minutes

Cooking Time: 1 hour and 20 minutes

Servings: 2 loaves

Ingredients:

- 1 ½ C. rye flour
- ½ C. pumpkin puree
- 2 eggs, whisked
- 3 Tbsp. sugar
- ½ C. almond milk, warm
- ½ C. psyllium husk powder
- 1 tsp. pumpkin pie spice
- 1 tsp. baking soda
- ½ tsp. salt

Directions:

1. In a bowl, mix the flour with sugar, husk powder, spices, salt, and baking soda and stir.
2. Add the rest of the ingredients, stir the mix well, pour into 2 loaf pans, and bake at 330 degrees °F for 1 hour and 20 minutes.
3. Cool down, slice, and serve.

Nutrition/ loaf: calories 212, fat 5.4, fiber 2.3, carbs 8.54, protein 4

SOFT RICE BREAD

Preparation Time: 10 minutes

Cooking Time: 1 hour and 10 minutes

Servings: 2 loaves

Ingredients:

- 1 ½ C. rice flour
- 1 tsp. salt
- 1 tsp. apple cider vinegar
- 1 tsp. baking soda
- 1 tsp. baking powder
- 3 Tbsp. psyllium husk powder
- 1 C. warm water
- 2 eggs, whisked
- 1 egg yolk, whisked
- Cooking spray

Directions:

1. In a large bowl, mix the rice flour with salt, baking powder and soda, and husk powder and stir.
2. Add the eggs and the remaining ingredients except for the cooking spray and stir until you obtain a dough.
3. Knead the dough for 10 minutes, transfer to 2 **loaf** pans greased with cooking spray, and bake at 350 degrees °F for 1 hour and 20 minutes.
4. Cool the bread down, slice, and serve.

Nutrition/ loaf: calories 172, fat 4.4, fiber 2.3, carbs 5.5, protein 2.3

SPINACH CORN BREAD

Preparation Time: 10 minutes

Cooking Time: 40 minutes

Servings: 2 loaves

Ingredients:

- 1 Tbsp. olive oil
- 1 tsp. salt
- ½ C. spinach, chopped
- 3 C. corn flour
- 1 C. warm water
- 1 tsp. baking soda
- 1 Tbsp. sugar
- ½ C. cheddar, shredded

Directions:

1. In a bowl, mix the flour with the baking soda, sugar, and other ingredients, and stir well until you obtain an elastic dough.
2. Transfer the dough to 2 loaf pans, bake at 390 degrees °F for 40 minutes, cool down, slice, and serve.

Nutrition/ loaf: Calories 300, fat 6.7, fiber 3.4, carbs 5.4, protein 4.9

WHEAT AND ALMOND FOCACCIA

Preparation Time: 2 hours

Cooking Time: 40 minutes

Servings: 2 focaccias

Ingredients:

- 1 C. wheat flour
- 1 C. almond flour
- ½ tsp. salt
- ½ tsp. cayenne pepper
- ½ C. olive oil
- 2 garlic cloves, minced
- 1 Tbsp. baking powder
- 5 eggs, whisked
- 1 Tbsp. rosemary, dried
- Cooking spray

Directions:

1. In a bowl, mix the wheat flour with the almond flour and the other ingredients except for the oil and stir well.
2. Add the oil gradually and stir everything well again.
3. Pour this into 2 square pans greased with the cooking spray, bake at 330 degrees °F for 40 minutes, cool down, and serve.

Nutrition/ focaccia: Calories 243, fat 5.4, fiber 4.4, carbs 5.4, protein 3.2

WHOLE WHEAT CAULIFLOWER BREAD

Preparation Time: 10 minutes

Cooking Time: 1 hour

Servings: 1 loaf

Ingredients:

- 5 Tbsp. olive oil
- 5 eggs, whisked
- 1 C. whole wheat flour
- 2 C. cauliflower, grated
- ½ tsp. salt
- 1 Tbsp. baking soda
- ½ tsp. black pepper

Directions:

1. In a bowl, mix the cauliflower with whole wheat flour and the other ingredients, stir, and knead for 10 minutes until you obtain an elastic dough.
2. Transfer the dough to a loaf pan and bake at 350 degrees °F for 1 hour.
3. Cool down, slice, and serve.

Nutrition/ loaf: Calories 287, fat 6.5, fiber 2.3, carbs 3.4, protein 5.4

EGGPLANT RYE BREAD

Preparation Time: 10 minutes

Cooking Time: 1 hour

Servings: 1 loaf

Ingredients:

- 2 Tbsp. sugar
- ½ C. warm milk
- 2 eggs, whisked
- 1 ½ C. rye flour
- 1 tsp. salt
- 2 eggplants, washed and grated
- 1 tsp. turmeric powder
- 2 tsp. baking powder

Directions:

1. In a bowl, mix the flour with the milk and the other ingredients, stir well, and transfer to a loaf pan.
2. Bake at 350 °F for 1 hour, cool down, slice, and serve.

Nutrition/ loaf: Calories 200, fat 4.4, fiber 3.3, carbs 7.5, protein 4.3

ONION CORN BREAD

Preparation Time: 1 hour

Cooking Time: 40 minutes

Servings: 1 loaf

Ingredients:

- 6 spring onions, chopped
- 2 Tbsp. olive oil
- 1 yellow onion, chopped
- 4 C. corn flour
- ½ tsp. salt
- ½ tsp. white pepper
- 1 ½ C. warm water
- 2 tsp. dry yeast

Directions:

1. In a bowl, mix the spring onions with the oil, flour, and the other ingredients, stir well, knead until you obtain a dough, cover the bowls, and leave aside for 1 hour.
2. Transfer to a loaf pan, bake the bread at 375 degrees °F for 40 minutes, cool down, slice, and serve.

Nutrition/ loaf: Calories 253, fat 4.4, fiber 2.3, carbs 7.4, protein 4.3

CHAPTER 5. ENRICHED FLAVOR RECIPES

SOURDOUGH ENGLISH ARTISAN BREAD

Preparation Time: 1 hour 10 minutes

Cooking Time: 40 mints

Serving: 1 loaf

Ingredients

- 2 Tbsp. sugar
- 6 C. all-purpose flour
- 2 C. warm water
- ¼ C. butter
- 1 C. sourdough starter
- 1 Tbsp. salt
- Cornmeal (for coating)

Directions:

1. In a large bowl, mix the salt, sugar, and flour together. Add the warm water, butter, and sourdough starter and mix until a dough forms.

2. Knead the dough on a floured surface for 10 minutes until it is smooth and elastic.

3. Place the dough in a lightly oiled bowl, cover it with a damp towel, and let it rise for 1 hour in a warm place.

4. Preheat the oven to 425°F.

5. Shape the dough into a round loaf and place it on a baking sheet dusted with cornmeal. Make shallow slashes on the top of the loaf.

6. Bake the bread for 40 minutes or until it is golden brown and sounds hollow when tapped.

7. Let the bread cool on a wire rack for at least 10 minutes before serving.

Nutrition: Calories 240, fat 7, fiber 4, carbs 12, protein 12

GERMAN BREAD

Preparation Time: 40 minutes

Cooking Time: 1 hour 15 minutes

Serving: 4

Ingredients

- 8 C. white rye flour
- 4 C. all-purpose flour
- 1 C. Sourdough starter
- 1-liter warm water
- 2 Tbsp. white sugar
- 2 Tbsp. salt
- 1 tsp. instant yeast

Directions:

1. In a large bowl, mix the rye flour, all-purpose flour, sugar, salt, yeast, and sourdough starter.
2. Gradually add the warm water and stir the mixture until a dough forms. You may not need to use all 1 liter of water.
3. Knead the dough for 15-20 minutes, either by hand or using a heavy-duty stand mixer, until it is smooth and elastic.
4. Place the dough in a large, oiled bowl, cover it with plastic wrap, and let it rise for 1 1/2 hours.
5. Transfer the dough to a floured surface and knead it for an additional 5 minutes.
6. Divide the dough into two equal portions and shape each into a loaf. Place the loaves in two greased 9x5-inch loaf pans. Let the loaves rise for another hour.
7. Preheat your oven to 440°F (220°C). Using a sharp knife, make 1/4-inch cuts on the surface of each loaf.
8. Bake the loaves for 45-60 minutes or until they are golden brown. Allow the bread to cool on a wire rack before serving.

Nutrition: Calories 210, fat 6 fiber 3, carbs 26, protein 5

BASIC ARTISAN SOURDOUGH BREAD

Preparation Time: 30 minutes, including rise time

Cooking Time: 1 hour 30 mints

Serving: 7

Ingredients:

- 3 ½ C. flour
- 2 tsp. salt
- 2 ½ C. sourdough starter
- 1 ½ C. water
- 2 g brown sugar (optional)
- Oil for greasing (flavorless)

Directions:

1. In a large mixing bowl, combine the flour, sourdough starter, water, and (optional) brown sugar. Mix until a sticky dough forms.

2. On a floured surface, knead the dough for 8-10 minutes until it is smooth and elastic. Add the salt to the dough and knead for an additional 2-3 minutes.

3. Place the dough in a greased bowl, cover it with a damp towel, and let it rise in a warm, draft-free area for 2-3 hours or until it has doubled in size.

4. Preheat your oven to 400°F (204°C). Lightly grease a 9x5-inch loaf pan with oil.

5. Gently deflate the dough and shape it into a loaf. Place it in the prepared loaf pan.

6. Using a sharp knife, make an X-shaped cut on the top of the loaf.

7. Bake the bread for 1 hour and 30 minutes, or until it is golden brown and sounds hollow when tapped on the bottom.

8. Allow the bread to cool on a wire rack before slicing and serving.

Nutrition: Calories 240, fat 7, fiber 4, carbs 12, protein 12

SOURDOUGH BANANA ARTISAN BREAD

Preparation Time: 15 minutes

Cooking Time: 1 hour

Serving: 5

Ingredients:

- ½ C. coconut oil or butter
- ¾ C. sugar
- 1-2 eggs
- 2 mashed bananas
- 1 tsp. vanilla extract
- 1 C. sourdough starter
- 1 and ¾ C. all-purpose flour
- 1 tsp. baking soda
- 1 tsp. baking powder
- 1 tsp. salt
- ¾ C. chocolate chips or chopped walnuts (optional)

Directions:

1. Using a bowl, combine the sourdough starter with sugar, vanilla, and eggs. Incorporate coconut oil or butter.

2. In another bowl, mix the mashed bananas with the sourdough mixture.

3. In a separate bowl, blend together the flour, baking soda, baking powder, and salt.

4. Add the dry ingredients to the banana mixture and knead well to form a dough.

5. If desired, fold in chocolate chips or chopped walnuts.

6. Load the batter into an oiled loaf pan and bake at 350ºF for 1 hour.

7. Allow the bread to cool on a wire rack before serving. You can also store it in the refrigerator for later use.

Nutrition: Calories 190, fat 8, fiber 4, carbs 32, protein 3

GLUTEN-FREE SOURDOUGH BREAD

Preparation Time: 45 minutes

Cooking Time: 16 hours

Serving: 8

Ingredients:

- 1 tsp. salt
- 4 tsp. olive oil/coconut oil/sunflower oil
- 1/5 tsp. honey
- 3 eggs
- 1 C. brown rice flour
- 1/3 C. buckwheat flour
- 1/3 C. millet flour
- 1/3 C. sorghum flour
- Brown rice sourdough starter
- 1 C. potato starch
- 1 C. sugar

Directions:

1. In a bowl, mix the same amount of sourdough starter, rice flour, and water (½ c.). Allow it to sit for 8-12 hours at room temperature.
2. In a separate bowl, combine whisked eggs, water, and coconut oil and separate the mixture into two. The mixture should be maintained warm.
3. Make a powder mixture of all the flours forming part of the ingredients in a bowl and add salt and sugar to mix. Combine this mixture with one part of the egg mixture and knead well.
4. Add the rice sourdough starter to the other part of the egg mixture and empty this to the kneaded dour. Knead some more to ensure a uniform mix, and let it sit to rise for 4 hours in plastic-covered pans.
5. Bake the bread in preheated oven.

Nutrition: Calories 170, fat 7, fiber 4, carbs 23, protein 11

COUNTRY BREAD

Preparation Time: 10 minutes,

Cook Time: 3 hours

Servings: 4

Ingredients*:*

- 1 C. bread flour
- 2 ½ C. all-purpose flour
- 1 ½ C. of lukewarm water
- 2 ½ tsp. yeast (instant or rapid)
- ¼ tsp. baking soda
- 1 ½ tsp. of sugar
- 1 Tbsp. + 1 tsp. olive oil
- 1 tsp. of salt

Directions:

1. Put everything in the pan of your bread machine.
2. Set the machine to white bread program and medium crust.
3. Hit the start button.
4. Transfer bread to a rack for cooling once done.

Nutrition: Calories 122, fat 4, fiber 2, carbs 17, protein 2

BAKED SOURDOUGH CROUTONS

Preparation Time: 1 hour

Cooking Time: 40 minutes

Servings: 1 loaf

Ingredients:

- 1/3 C. butter, melted
- 1 1/2 tsp. Italian seasoning
- 1/4 tsp. extra-virgin olive oil
- 1/4 tsp. kosher salt
- 6 slices sourdough bread, cut into 1/2-inch cubes
- 2 tsp. grated parmesan cheese

Directions:

1. Set oven to 300 degrees °F.
2. Sauté bread pieces with all remaining ingredients and toss well.
3. Arrange on a baking sheet and bake for about 20 minutes.

Nutrition: Calories: 287; Total fat: 12g; Carbs: 41g; Fiber: 6g; Protein: 8g

HONEY SOURDOUGH LOAF

Preparation Time: 1 hour

Cooking Time: 40 minutes

Servings: 1 loaf

Ingredients:

- 2/3 C. liquid sourdough starter
- 1/2 C. water
- 1 Tbsp. vegetable oil
- 2 Tbsp. honey
- 1/2 tsp. salt
- 1/2 C. high protein wheat flour
- 2 C. bread flour

Directions:

1. Place all ingredients in the bread machine in the order specified by the manufacturer.
2. Choose the white bread cycle and press start.
3. Once the cycle is complete, take the bread out of the machine and place it on a wire rack to cool completely.
4. Once cooled, slice and serve. Enjoy your fresh homemade bread!

Nutrition: calories: 287; Total fat: 12g; Carbs: 41g; Fiber: 6g; Protein: 8g

MAPLE SOURDOUGH BREAD

Preparation Time: 2 hours

Cooking Time: 40 minutes

Servings: 6

Ingredients:

- 2/3 C. liquid sourdough starter
- 1/2 C. water
- 1 Tbsp. vegetable oil
- 2 Tbsp. bread
- 1/2 tsp. salt
- 1/2 C. high protein wheat flour
- 2 C. bread flour

Directions:

1. Place all ingredients in the bread machine in the order specified by the manufacturer.
2. Choose the white bread cycle and press start.
3. Once the cycle is complete, take the bread out of the machine and place it on a wire rack to cool completely.
4. Once cooled, slice and serve. Enjoy your fresh homemade bread!

Nutrition: Calories: 208; Fat: 8g; Carbs: 33.2g; Protein: 3.6g

RYE AND SOURDOUGH BAGUETTE

Preparation Time: 12 hours

Cooking Time: 40 minutes

Servings: 8

Ingredients:

- 1 C. rye flour
- 1½ C. bread flour
- 2/3 C. water
- 1/4 C. water
- 1/2 Tbsp. salt
- 1 Tbsp. white sugar
- 1 Tbsp. olive oil
- 1 Tbsp. caraway seed
- 1 C. sourdough starter

Directions:

1. In a large bowl, mix together 1 cup of rye flour, 1/2 cup of bread flour, and 2/3 cup of warm water. Cover the bowl with plastic wrap and let it rest at room temperature overnight.

2. Add 1/4 cup of warm water, sugar, oil, caraway seed, and salt to the bowl. Mix until well combined.

3. Gradually add in the remaining bread flour and mix until a soft dough forms.

4. Turn the dough out onto a lightly floured surface and knead for about 10 minutes until the dough is smooth and elastic.

5. Place the dough in a greased bowl, cover it with plastic wrap, and let it rise in a warm place until it has doubled in size (about 1 to 2 hours).

6. Punch down the dough. Divide the dough into 8 equal portions and shape each into a baguette. Place the baguettes onto a baking sheet lined with parchment paper.

7. Cover the baguettes with a clean, damp cloth and let them rise for another 30 minutes to 1 hour.

8. Preheat the oven to 425°F (220°C). Bake the baguettes for about 40.

9. Remove the baguettes from the oven and let them cool on a wire rack for at least 15 minutes before serving. Enjoy!

Nutrition: Calories 46 Fat 3.3 g Carbohydrate 2.7 g Protein 1.6 g

Tacos Calories 410 Carbohydrate 58.1g Protein 12.2 g

SOURDOUGH BREAKFAST SCONES

Preparation Time: 12 Hours

Cooking Time: 40 minutes

Servings: 1 loaf

Ingredients:

- 2 1/2 C. bread flour
- 1/2 tsp. salt
- 1 tsp. cream of tartar
- 1 tsp. baking soda
- 1/2 C. white sugar
- 1 tsp. apple pie spice
- 1/3 C. cold butter
- 1 1/4 C. sourdough starter
- 2 Tbsp. milk (optional)
- Coarse sugar, for garnish (optional)

Directions:

1. Set oven to 400 degrees.
2. Combine cream of tartar, baking soda, sugar, flour, salt, and apple pie spice in a bowl.
3. Add butter and mix together well.
4. Add a starter and knead to form a soft dough.
5. Divide into several equal pieces and brush the tops with milk and sugar.
6. Bake for 15 minutes until golden brown.

Nutrition: Calories 200 Fat 13 g Protein 5 g Carbohydrates 18 g

SOURDOUGH OLIVE LOAF

Preparation Time: 1 hour

Cooking Time: 40 minutes

Servings: 6

Ingredients:

- 2 1/2 C. warm water
- 1 1/4 C. sourdough starter
- 1 tsp. molasses
- 2 Tbsp. olive oil
- 1 Tbsp. salt
- 7 1/2 C. bread flour
- 1 C. kalamata olives, pitted and chopped
- 2 Tbsp. chopped fresh rosemary
- 1 Tbsp. sesame seeds

Directions:

1. Combine water and molasses.
2. Add salt and olive oil and mix well; add flour one C. at a Time and continue mixing.
3. Add herbs and olives.
4. Place dough on a floured surface and knead.
5. Place in a greased bowl and cover with a towel. Allow rising for about an hour.
6. Punch down to remove air once ready and divide into two loaves.
7. Spray cold water on the loaves and sprinkle with sesame seeds. Cover and allow to rise for half an hour.
8. Bake at 400 degrees for half an hour.

Nutrition: Calories 200 Fat 13 g Protein 5 g Carbohydrates 18 g

POPPY SEED SOURDOUGH LOAF

Preparation Time: 1 hour

Cooking Time: 40 minutes

Servings: 6 loaves

Ingredients:

- 3/4 lb. butter
- 1 large onion, minced
- 2 Tbsp. poppy seeds, or to taste
- 1 loaf sourdough French bread
- 1 lb. white American cheese, sliced

Directions:

1. Set oven to 350 degrees.
2. Sauté onions in butter until tender and fragrant.
3. Add seeds and mix well over low heat.
4. Slice diagonal slits onto the top of the bread.
5. Place a slice of cheese in between the slits and drizzle the butter mixture into it.
6. Wrap tightly with foil and bake for half an hour.

Nutrition: Calories 153 Fat 9 g Carbohydrates 10 g Protein 9 g

STILTON AND CILANTRO SOURDOUGH LOAF

Preparation Time: 1 hour 30 minutes

Cooking Time: 40 minutes

Servings: 7

Ingredients:

- 3/4 lb. butter
- A handful of cilantro, diced
- 1 large onion, minced
- 1 loaf sourdough French bread
- 1 lb. stilton cheese, sliced

Directions:

1. Set oven to 350 degrees.
2. Sauté onions in butter until tender and fragrant.
3. Slice diagonal slits onto the top of the bread.
4. Place a slice of cheese and sprinkle cilantro in between the slits and drizzle butter mixture into it.
5. Wrap tightly with foil and bake for half an hour.

Nutrition: Calories 153 Fat 9 g Carbohydrates 10 g Protein 9 g

CHEESY HERBED SOURDOUGH LOAF

Preparation Time: 1 hour

Cooking Time: 40 minutes

Servings: 1 loaf

Ingredients:

- 3/4 lb. butter
- 1 C. of dried herbs (rosemary, dill, basil, oregano)
- 1 (1 lb.) loaf of sourdough French bread
- 1 lb. white American cheese, sliced

Directions:

1. Set oven to 350 degrees.
2. Sauté herbs in butter until tender and fragrant.
3. Slice diagonal slits onto the top of the bread.
4. Place a slice of cheese in between the slits and drizzle the herb mixture into it.
5. Wrap tightly with foil and bake for half an hour.

Nutrition: Calories 165, fat 5, fiber 6, carbs 22, protein 5

GARLIC HERBED BUTTER SOURDOUGH LOAF

Preparation Time: 1 hour

Cooking Time: 40 minutes

Servings: 1 loaf

Ingredients:

- 3/4 lb. butter
- 1 Tbsp. garlic powder
- 1 C. dried herbs of choice
- 1 loaf sourdough French bread

Directions:

1. Set oven to 350 degrees.
2. Sauté butter with garlic powder and herbs.
3. Slice diagonal slits onto the top of the bread.
4. Drizzle the butter mixture into the slits.
5. Wrap tightly with foil and bake for half an hour.

Nutrition: Calories 165, fat 5, fiber 6, carbs 22, protein 5

ONION AND CHIVE SOURDOUGH BREAD

Preparation Time: 1 hour

Cooking Time: 40 minutes

Servings: 6

Ingredients:

- 3/4 lb. butter
- 1 large onion, minced
- 1/2 C. chives, diced
- 1 (1 lb.) loaf of sourdough French bread
- 1 pack of cream cheese, softened

Directions:

1. Set oven to 350 degrees.
2. Sauté onions in butter until tender and fragrant.
3. Mix chives together with cream cheese.
4. Slice diagonal slits onto the top of the bread.
5. Scoop cream cheese mixture in between the slits and drizzle onion mixture.
6. Wrap tightly with foil and bake for half an hour.

Nutrition: Calories 439 Fat 3.1 g Carbohydrates 80.1 g Protein 24.9 g

SESAME SOURDOUGH LOAF

Preparation Time: 2 hours

Cooking Time: 49 minutes

Servings: 1 loaf

Ingredients:

- 3/4 lb. butter
- 3 Tbsp. sesame seeds
- 2 Tbsp. sesame oil
- 1 loaf sourdough French bread

Directions:

1. Set oven to 350 degrees.
2. Sauté sesame seeds in butter until tender and fragrant.
3. Add sesame oil and mix well over low heat.
4. Slice diagonal slits onto the top of the bread.
5. Drizzle butter mixture into it.
6. Wrap tightly with foil and bake for half an hour.

Nutrition: Calories 439 Fat 3.1 g Carbohydrates 80.1 g Protein 24.9 g

CHEESY GARLIC SOURDOUGH LOAF

Preparation Time: 1 hour

Cooking Time: 40 minutes

Servings: 1 loaf

Ingredients:

- 3/4 lb. butter
- 2 cloves garlic, diced
- 2 Tbsp. garlic powder
- 1 (1 lb.) loaf of sourdough French bread
- 1 lb. white American cheese, sliced

Directions:

1. Set oven to 350 degrees.
2. Sauté garlic in butter until tender and fragrant.
3. Slice diagonal slits onto the top of the bread.
4. Place a slice of cheese in between the slits and drizzle the butter mixture into it.
5. Wrap tightly with foil and bake for half an hour.

Nutrition: Calories 388 Fat 12.8 g Carbohydrates 54.8 g Protein 17.3 g

POTATO ROLLS

Preparation Time: 55 minutes

Cooking Time: 20 minutes

Servings: 24 pieces

Ingredients:

- 2 sweet potatoes, cooked, peeled, and mashed
- 1 C. milk
- 3 Tbsp. butter, soft
- 4 C. white flour
- 1 egg, whisked
- 1 tsp. salt
- 2 tsp. dry yeast

Directions:

1. In the bread machine, combine the sweet potatoes with the milk and the other ingredients and use the basil dough cycle.
2. At the end of this cycle, tear pieces of the dough, shape medium balls, and arrange them on a lined baking sheet.
3. Leave the dough to rise for 45 minutes and then bake at 375 degrees °F for 20 minutes.

Nutrition/roll: Calories 141, fat 6, fiber 3, carbs 17, protein 4

TASTY PRETZELS

Preparation Time: 20 minutes

Cooking Time: 10 minutes

Servings: 12

Ingredients:

- 1 Tbsp. sugar
- 3 C. white flour
- 2 tsp. dry yeast
- 1 and ½ C. water+ 2 quarts
- 1 tsp. salt
- 1/3 C. baking soda

Directions:

1. In your bread machine, mix the sugar with flour, yeast, 1 and ½ C. water, and salt and set the machine to dough cycle.
2. When the cycle is done, transfer the dough to a floured working surface, knead, divide it into 12 pieces, and roll each piece into a rope.
3. Heat up a pan with the rest of the water and the baking soda, bring to a simmer over medium heat, add the pretzels, simmer for 2 minutes, and transfer them to lined baking sheets.
4. Bake at 475 degrees °F for 10 minutes.

Nutrition/ pretzel: Calories 40, fat 2, fiber 2, carbs 6, protein 1

PIZZA DOUGH

Preparation Time: 10 minutes

Cooking Time: 15 minutes

Servings: 2 pizzas

Ingredients:

- 2 Tbsp. olive oil
- 4 C. bread flour
- 1 and ½ C. water
- 1 Tbsp. sugar
- 2 tsp. salt
- 2 tsp. active yeast

Directions:

1. In a large mixing bowl, combine the flour, sugar, salt, and yeast. Add the water and olive oil, and mix until a shaggy dough forms.

2. Knead the dough for 5-10 minutes until it becomes smooth and elastic. Cover the bowl with a clean towel or plastic wrap, and let the dough rise for 1-2 hours until it doubles in size.

3. Preheat your oven to the highest temperature possible (usually 500-550 degrees °F). If you have a pizza stone, place it in the oven to preheat.

4. Divide the dough into 2 equal portions. On a floured surface, roll out each portion into a 12-inch circle. Transfer the dough to a pizza peel or a baking sheet lined with parchment paper.

5. Add your desired toppings. Bake the pizza in the preheated oven for 10-15 minutes or until the crust is crispy and the cheese is melted and bubbly.

6. Remove the pizza from the oven and let it cool for a few minutes before slicing and serving.

Nutrition/ pizza crust: Calories 40, fat 2, fiber 2, carbs 5, protein 1

BUTTER BREAD

Preparation Time: 10 minutes

Cooking Time: 40 minutes

Servings: 1 loaf

Ingredients:

- 1 cup sourdough starter at room temperature
- 1/2 cup (1 stick) unsalted butter, softened
- 3 cups bread flour
- 1 teaspoon salt
- 1/4 cup warm water
- 2 tablespoons brown sugar

Directions:

1. In a large mixing bowl, combine the sourdough starter, softened butter, flour, and salt. Mix until a shaggy dough forms.

2. In a small bowl, dissolve the brown sugar in warm water. Add this mixture to the dough and knead for 10-15 minutes until the dough is smooth and elastic.

3. Cover the bowl with a clean towel or plastic wrap, and let the dough rise for 6-12 hours until it doubles in size.

4. Preheat your oven to 375 degrees F. Grease a 9x5-inch loaf pan.

5. Punch down the dough and shape it into a loaf. Place the loaf in the prepared pan and let it rise for another 30 minutes.

6. Bake the bread for 35-40 minutes, or until the crust is golden brown and the bread sounds hollow when tapped on the bottom.

7. Remove the bread from the oven and let it cool in the pan for 5-10 minutes. Transfer the bread to a wire rack to cool completely before slicing and serving.

Nutrition/ slice: calories 152, fat 4, fiber 2, carbs 15, protein 4

MILK ONION SAVORY BREAD

Preparation Time: 20 minutes

Cooking Time: 2 hours

Servings: 1 loaf

Ingredients:

- 2 Tbsp. coconut oil, melted
- 2 tsp. salt
- 1 and ½ C. water
- 1 Tbsp. sugar
- 4 C. white flour
- 2 Tbsp. dry milk
- 2 tsp. active yeast
- 4 Tbsp. dry onion soup mix

Directions:

1. Combine all the ingredients in your bread machine, select the bread cycle and medium crust, and start the machine.
2. Cool the bread down before serving.

Nutrition/ slice: calories 152, fat 4, fiber 3, carbs 15, protein 7

PARMESAN BREAD

Preparation Time: 10 minutes

Cooking Time: 45-50 mints

Servings: 1 loaf

Ingredients:

- 1 cup sourdough starter at room temperature
- 2 tablespoons avocado oil
- 3 garlic cloves, minced
- 1 and 1/2 cups warm water
- 3 tablespoons fresh chives, chopped
- 1 tablespoon fresh basil, chopped
- 1 teaspoon salt
- 1 tablespoon brown sugar
- 2 cups bread flour
- 2 cups all-purpose flour
- 1/2 cup grated Parmesan cheese

Directions:

1. In a large mixing bowl, combine the sourdough starter, avocado oil, minced garlic, warm water, chives, basil, salt, and brown sugar. Mix well.

2. Gradually add in the bread flour and all-purpose flour, stirring until a shaggy dough forms.

3. Turn the dough out onto a floured surface and knead for 10-15 minutes until the dough is smooth and elastic.

4. Place the dough in a greased bowl, cover it with a towel or plastic wrap, and let it rise for 6-8 hours until it has doubled in size.

5. Preheat your oven to 375 degrees F. Grease a 9x5-inch loaf pan.

6. Punch down the dough and shape it into a loaf. Place the loaf in the prepared pan and let it rise for another 30-60 minutes.

7. Sprinkle the grated Parmesan cheese over the top of the bread.

8. Bake the bread for 45-50 minutes, or until the crust is golden brown and the bread sounds hollow when tapped on the bottom.

9. Remove the bread from the oven and let it cool in the pan for 5-10 minutes. Transfer the bread to a wire rack to cool completely before slicing and serving.

Nutrition/ slice: calories 102, fat 3, fiber 4, carbs 13, protein 4

JEWISH BREAD

Preparation Time: 2 hours and 10 minutes

Cooking Time: 1 hour

Servings: 1 bread

Ingredients:

- 1 egg yolk, whisked
- 1 egg white, whisked
- 2 tsp. salt
- 1 C. warm water
- ½ C. honey
- 2 Tbsp. olive oil
- 4 C. white flour
- 2 tsp. bread machine yeast

Directions:

1. In your bread machine, mix the flour with yeast and the other ingredients, set the machine on basil cycle and light crust, and start the machine.
2. When the final rise is done, set the machine on pause, transfer the dough to a floured working surface, and knead gently.
3. Divide the dough into 3 parts, roll each part into long ropes, braid them together, and tuck the ends.
4. Transfer the bread to the bread machine and continue the cycle.
5. Cool down and serve.

Nutrition/ loaf: Calories 200, fat 7, fiber 3, carbs 20, protein 7

ITALIAN BREAD

Preparation Time: 10 minutes

Cooking Time: 1 hour

Servings: 1 loaf

Ingredients:

- 4 garlic cloves, minced
- 3 Tbsp. soft butter
- 1 bulb roasted garlic
- 1 C. milk
- ½ C. cheddar, grated
- 3 C. white bread flour
- 1 tsp. salt
- 2 Tbsp. sugar
- 1 tsp. garlic powder
- 1 tsp. dry active yeast

Directions:

1. Squeeze roasted garlic, mash the flesh, and put it in a bowl.
2. In your bread machine, mix all the other ingredients, set the machine on basic white cycle and medium crust, and start the program.
3. When the last kneading cycle starts, add the roasted garlic as well.
4. Make the bread and cool down before serving.

Nutrition/ slice: calories 140, fat 4, fiber 3, carbs 16, protein 4

VEGGIE BREAD

Preparation Time: 10 minutes

Cooking Time: 2 hours

Servings: 1 loaf

Ingredients:

- ¼ C. spring onions, chopped
- ½ C. water
- ¼ C. green bell pepper, chopped
- 2 Tbsp. chives, chopped
- 2 C. white flour
- 1 Tbsp. butter
- 1 tsp. creole seasoning
- 1 Tbsp. sugar
- 1 tsp. salt
- 1 tsp. active dry yeast

Directions:

1. In the bread machine, mix all the ingredients, select the white bread cycle and medium crust, and start the machine.
2. Cool the bread down and serve.

Nutrition/ slice: calories 47, fat 3, fiber 3, carbs 7, protein 1

OATMEAL BREAD

Preparation Time: 10 minutes

Cooking Time: 2 hours and 30 minutes

Servings: 1 loaf

Ingredients:

- 2 tsp. salt
- 2 Tbsp. butter, soft
- 1 C. warm water
- 3 Tbsp. honey
- 1 Tbsp. molasses
- ½ C. old-fashioned oats
- 1 egg, whisked
- 2 tsp. dry yeast

Directions:

1. In your bread machine, mix all the ingredients.
2. Set the machine on white bread cycle and medium crust and push the start button.
3. When the bread is done, cool down and serve.

Nutrition/ slice: calories 162, fat 7, fiber 4, carbs 17, protein 5

ROMANO CHEESE BREAD

Preparation Time: 10 minutes

Cooking Time: 2 hours

Servings: 1 loaf

Ingredients:

- 1 C. water
- ½ C. Romano cheese, shredded
- 3 C. white flour
- 1 Tbsp. oregano, chopped
- 2 Tbsp. sugar
- 1 tsp. salt
- 1 tsp. black pepper
- 2 tsp. active yeast
- 2 Tbsp. olive oil

Directions:

1. In your bread machine, mix the flour and the other ingredients, select the white bread cycle and light crust, and push the start button.
2. Cool the bread down, slice, and serve.

Nutrition/slice: calories 70, fat 3, fiber 3, carbs 7, protein 2

CHEDDAR, OLIVES AND TOMATO BREAD

Preparation Time: 10 minutes

Cooking Time: 1 hour

Servings: 1 loaf

Ingredients:

- ½ C. cheddar cheese, grated
- 3 Tbsp. black olives, pitted and sliced
- ½ C. sun-dried tomatoes, chopped
- 3 Tbsp. soft butter
- 1 C. milk
- 3 C. white bread flour
- 1 tsp. salt
- 2 Tbsp. sugar
- 1 tsp. dry active yeast

Directions:

1. In your bread machine, mix the cheese with the olives and the other ingredients, set the machine on basic white cycle and medium crust, and start the program.
2. Make the bread and cool down before serving.

Nutrition/ slice: calories 130, fat 3.2, fiber 3, carbs 11.6, protein 4

PARMESAN AND CUCUMBER BREAD

Preparation Time: 10 minutes

Cooking Time: 2 hours

Servings: 1 loaf

Ingredients:

- 2 Tbsp. olive oil
- ½ C. parmesan, grated
- 1 C. cucumber, minced
- 1 and ½ C. water, warm
- 1 tsp. salt
- 2 tsp. active dry yeast
- 4 C. white flour

Directions:

1. In your bread machine, combine all the ingredients, select the basil cycle and medium crust, bake, cool down, and serve.

Nutrition/ slice: calories 132, fat 4.5, fiber 3.2, carbs 13, protein 4

SPRING ONIONS AND ZUCCHINI BREAD

Preparation Time: 10 minutes

Cooking Time: 1 hour

Servings: 1 loaf

Ingredients:

- ½ C. spring onions, chopped
- ½ C. water
- ½ C. zucchini, chopped
- 3 C. bread flour
- 1 Tbsp. olive oil
- 1 tsp. salt
- 1 tsp. active dry yeast

Directions:

1. In the bread machine, mix all the ingredients, select the white bread cycle and medium crust, and start the machine.
2. Cool the bread down and serve.

Nutrition/ slice: calories 87, fat 6.5, fiber 3, carbs 7, protein 3.4

MILK AND BASIL BREAD

Preparation Time: 10 minutes

Cooking Time: 2 hours

Servings: 1 loaf

Ingredients:

- 1 C. almond milk
- 1 Tbsp. sugar
- 1 Tbsp. basil, chopped
- 3 Tbsp. butter, soft
- 3 C. bread flour
- 1 tsp. salt
- 2 tsp. dry machine yeast

Directions:

1. In the bread machine, mix the milk with the sugar and the other ingredients, choose the white bread setting and medium crust, and start the machine.
2. Cool down and serve.

Nutrition/ slice: calories 100, fat 3, fiber 4, carbs 7, protein 3

MINT BREAD

Preparation Time: 10 minutes

Cooking Time: 2 hours

Servings: 1 loaf

Ingredients:

- 1 C. warm water
- 1 Tbsp. mint, chopped
- 3 Tbsp. honey
- 3 Tbsp. coconut oil, melted
- 3 and ½ C. white flour
- 1 tsp. salt
- 2 tsp. dry machine yeast

Directions:

1. In the bread machine, mix the warm water with mint and the other ingredients, select the white bread setting and medium crust, and start the machine.
2. Cool down and serve.

Nutrition/ slice: calories 70, fat 3, fiber 2.3, carbs 7, protein 2

CHAPTER 6. SANDWICH BREADS RECIPES

GARLIC SANDWICH BREAD

Preparation Time: 2 hours

Cooking Time: 40 minutes

Servings: 1 loaf

Ingredients:

- 1 C. hot water
- 2 Tbsp. sugar
- 2 tsp. dry yeast
- ¼ C. avocado oil
- 3 garlic cloves, minced
- 4 C. coconut flour
- ½ tsp. coriander, ground
- ½ tsp. rosemary, dried
- 2 Tbsp. butter, melted
- ½ tsp. turmeric powder

Directions:

1. In a large bowl, mix the flour with the garlic, coriander, and the other ingredients except for the water and the oil, and stir well.
2. Add the water and the oil gradually and knead the dough for 10 minutes.
3. Leave the dough covered to rise for 1 hour and 30 minutes in a warm place.
4. Transfer the dough to a loaf pan, leave it to rise for 30 minutes more, and bake at 370 degrees °F for 40 minutes.

Nutrition/ slice: calories 233, fat 6, fiber 2, carbs 38, protein 5

WHOLE GRAIN SANDWICH BREAD

Preparation Time: 1 hour and 30 minutes

Cooking Time: 30 minutes

Servings: 2 loaves

Ingredients:

- 6 C. whole wheat flour
- 1 Tbsp. dry active yeast
- ¼ C. honey
- ¼ C. olive oil
- 1 and ½ Tbsp. wheat gluten
- 2 tsp. salt
- 2 and ½ C. warm water
- ½ tsp. turmeric powder
- ½ tsp. nutmeg, ground

Directions:

1. In a bowl, mix the water with the yeast and 2 C. flour, stir, and leave aside for 20 minutes.
2. Add the rest of the ingredients and stir until you obtain a dough.
3. Knead the dough for 10 minutes, cover the bowl, and leave aside to rise for 1 hour.
4. Divide the dough into 2 loaf pans and leave them to rise for 10 more minutes.
5. Bake at 360 degrees °F for 30 minutes, cool down, and serve.

Nutrition/ slice: calories 110, fat 2.4, fiber 0.7, carbs 18.2, protein 2.3

SOURDOUGH SPELT SANDWICH BREAD

Preparation Time: 5 hours

Cooking Time: 40 minutes

Servings: 1 loaf

Ingredients:

- 8 oz. sourdough starter
- 3 C. whole spelt flour
- 1 C. white flour
- 2 Tbsp. maple syrup
- 2 Tbsp. olive oil
- 1 C. water
- 1 tsp. salt

Directions:

1. In a bowl, mix the sourdough starter with the flour and the other ingredients, stir well, and knead until you obtain a dough.
2. Knead the dough for 10 minutes, cover it with plastic wrap, and leave aside to rise for 4 hours and 30 minutes.
3. Transfer to a loaf pan, leave aside to rise for 30 minutes more, and bake at 360 degrees °F for 40 minutes.
4. Cool down and serve.

Nutrition/ loaf: Calories 253, fat 4.4, fiber 2, carbs 25, protein 5.4

CHEESY SANDWICH BREAD

Preparation Time: 3 hours

Cooking Time: 30 minutes

Servings: 1 loaf

Ingredients:

- 1 C. zucchini, shredded
- 1 and ½ tsp. dry instant yeast
- 2 Tbsp. sugar
- 1 C. warm water
- 3 and ½ C. white flour
- 1 tsp. salt
- ½ C. red onion, chopped
- 1 C. cheddar cheese, shredded

Directions:

1. In a bowl, mix the flour with the yeast, sugar, and half of the water, stir, and leave aside for 30 minutes.
2. Add the rest of the ingredients and stir until you obtain a dough; knead for 10 minutes, cover the bowl, and leave aside for 2 hours.
3. Transfer to a loaf pan, leave the dough to rise for 30 minutes more, and bake at 370 degrees °F for 30 minutes.
4. Cool down before serving.

Nutrition/slice: Calories 223, fat 5.4, fiber 4.5, carbs 14, protein 3.4

TOMATO SANDWICH BREAD

Preparation Time: 2 hours

Cooking Time: 35 minutes

Servings: 2 loaves

Ingredients:

- 6 C. white flour
- 1 oz. dry yeast
- 2 Tbsp. sugar
- 1 tsp. salt
- ½ tsp. basil, dried
- ½ tsp. rosemary, dried
- 2 C. tomato juice
- ½ C. tomato sauce
- 1 tsp. oregano, dried
- 1 tsp. garlic powder
- 2 Tbsp. olive oil

Directions:

1. In a bowl, mix half of the flour with the yeast, sugar, salt, and tomato juice, stir and leave aside for 30 minutes.
2. Add the rest of the ingredients gradually and stir until you obtain a dough.
3. Knead the dough for 10 minutes, cover the bowl, and leave aside for 1 hour to rise.
4. Transfer the dough to 2 loaves pan, leave the dough to rise for 30 minutes more, and bake at 360 degrees °F for 35 minutes.
5. Cool the bread down, slice, and serve.

Nutrition/ slice: calories 102, fat 1, fiber 1, carbs 20, protein 3

VEGAN SANDWICH BREAD

Preparation Time: 1 hour and 30 minutes

Cooking Time: 45 minutes

Servings: 1 loaf

Ingredients:

- ½ C. warm water
- 2 Tbsp. agave syrup
- ½ C. almond milk
- 1 Tbsp. dry active yeast
- 3 C. organic almond flour
- 1 tsp. salt
- 1 tsp. sweet paprika
- 1 tsp. turmeric powder

Directions:

1. In a bowl, mix the yeast with agave syrup and water, stir and leave aside for 10 minutes.
2. In another bowl, mix the flour with salt, paprika, and turmeric and stir.
3. Add yeast mix, also add the milk, stir until you obtain a dough, and leave aside to rise covered for 1 hour and 20 minutes.
4. Transfer to a loaf pan, leave the dough to rise for 10 minutes more, and bake at 350 degrees °F for 45 minutes.
5. Cool down, slice, and serve.

Nutrition/ slice: calories 206, fat 4, fiber 1, carbs 35, protein 4

SPROUTED BREAD SANDWICH

Preparation Time: 10 minutes

Cooking Time: 45 minutes

Servings: 2 loaves

Ingredients:

- 6 C. sprouted wheat flour
- 2 tsp. salt
- 3 Tbsp. honey
- 3 C. buttermilk
- 3 Tbsp. coconut oil, melted
- 1 Tbsp. butter, soft
- 1 tsp. cumin, ground

Directions:

1. In a bowl, mix the flour with salt, honey, and the other ingredients, stir until you obtain an elastic dough, knead for 10 minutes, and divide into 2 loaf pans.
2. Bake at 360 degrees °F for 45 minutes, cool down, and serve.

Nutrition/ slice: calories 201, fat 4.5, fiber 2.3, carbs 20, protein 4

DIABETIC SANDWICH BREAD

Preparation Time: 10 minutes

Cooking Time: 25 minutes

Servings: 1 loaf

Ingredients:

- 1 and ½ C. almond flour
- 3 Tbsp. butter, soft
- 1 tsp. salt
- 3 tsp. baking powder
- ½ tsp. cream of tartar
- 6 eggs, whisked
- Cooking spray

Directions:

1. In a bowl, mix the flour with melted butter and the other ingredients except for the cooking spray, stir well, and transfer to a loaf pan greased with cooking spray.
2. Bake at 375 degrees °F for 25 minutes, cool down, and serve.

Nutrition/ slice: calories 225, fat 20, fiber 2.3, carbs 0.8, protein 9.3

YOGURT SANDWICH BREAD

Preparation Time: 1 hour

Cooking Time: 40 minutes

Servings: 1 loaf

Ingredients:

- 1 and ½ C. warm water
- 1 C. natural yogurt
- 1 tsp. dry active yeast
- 1 tsp. salt
- 3 and ½ C. white flour

Directions:

1. In a bowl, mix the yeast with 1 C. flour and 1 C. water, stir, and leave aside for 10 minutes.
2. Add the rest of the ingredients, stir well, and knead until you obtain a dough.
3. Leave aside the dough to rise for 1 hour, transfer to a loaf pan and bake at 425 degrees °F for 40 minutes.

Nutrition/ slice: calories 161, fat 1, fiber 1, carbs 33, protein 5

ARTICHOKE SANDWICH BREAD

Preparation Time: 20 minutes

Cooking Time: 30 minutes

Servings: 1 loaf

Ingredients:

- 10 oz. canned artichoke hearts, drained and minced
- 1 C. parmesan, grated
- 2 garlic cloves, minced
- 1 tsp. baking soda
- 1 tsp. active dry yeast
- 2 and ½ C. almond flour
- 1 and ½ C. warm water
- 1 tsp. basil, dried

Directions:

1. In a bowl, mix the flour with baking soda, yeast, and 1.2 C. water, stir and leave aside for 15 minutes.
2. Add the rest of the ingredients and stir until you obtain a dough.
3. Knead the dough, transfer it to a loaf pan, and bake at 360 degrees °F for 30 minutes.

Nutrition/ slice: calories 211, fat 5, fiber 2, carbs 3.4, protein 4.3

KETOGENIC SANDWICH BREAD

Preparation Time: 10 minutes

Cooking Time: 25 minutes

Servings: 1 loaf

Ingredients:

- 2 and ½ C. coconut flour
- 2 C. whey protein
- ½ tsp. instant yeast
- 2 tsp. baking powder
- 1 and ¼ C. warm water
- 1 tsp. salt

Directions:

1. Take a bowl and mix the flour with the protein, yeast, baking powder, and salt, stir and leave aside for 10 minutes.
2. Add the water, stir until you obtain a dough, transfer it to a loaf pan, and bake at 400 degrees °F for 25 minutes.
3. Cool the bread down, slice, and serve.

Nutrition/ slice: calories 192, fat 12, fiber 3, carbs 8, protein 18

CORNBREAD SANDWICH BREAD

Preparation Time: 1 hour and 30 minutes

Cooking Time: 45 minutes

Servings: 1 loaf

Ingredients:

- ¼ C. honey
- 1 C. cornmeal
- 3 C. white flour
- 1 C. whole milk
- 3 Tbsp. vegetable oil
- 1 tsp. salt
- 2 tsp. dry yeast

Directions:

1. In a pan, combine the honey with milk and oil, whisk well, heat up over medium heat for 5 minutes, and take off the heat.
2. In a bowl, mix the flour with yeast, salt, and honey mix, stir well, and leave aside for 5 minutes.
3. Add the rest of the ingredients and stir until you obtain a dough, and then knead it for 10 minutes until smooth.
4. Cover the dough with plastic wrap and leave it in a warm place for 1 hour.
5. Transfer to a loaf pan, leave it to rise for 30 minutes more, and then bake at 375 degrees °F for 45 minutes.

Nutrition/ slice: calories 391, fat 6, fiber 4, carbs 48, protein 11

OLIVES SANDWICH BREAD

Preparation Time: 2 hours and 30 minutes

Cooking Time: 30 minutes

Servings: 1 loaf

Ingredients:

- 3 C. all-purpose flour
- 2 tsp. instant yeast
- 1 C. warm water
- 1 tsp. salt
- ½ tsp. turmeric powder
- ½ tsp. garlic powder
- ½ C. kalamata olives, pitted and chopped
- ½ Tbsp. olive oil

Directions:

1. In a bowl, mix the flour with the yeast and the other ingredients except for the water and stir well.
2. Add the water gradually, stir, and knead for 10 minutes until you obtain an elastic dough.
3. Cover the dough with plastic wrap and leave aside to rise for 1 hour in a warm place.
4. Transfer to a loaf pan and leave aside to rise for 1 more hour.
5. Bake at 375 degrees °F for 30 minutes, cool down, and serve.

Nutrition/ slice: calories 150, fat 3, fiber 1, carbs 26, protein 4.1

CHAPTER 7. SWEETS RECIPES

LEMON RHUBARB BREAD

Preparation Time: 10 minutes

Cooking Time: 40 minutes

Servings: 2 loaves

Ingredients:

- 1 C. almond milk
- 1 tsp. vanilla extract
- 1 Tbsp. lemon juice
- 2/3 C. vegetable oil
- 2 eggs, whisked
- 1 C. sugar
- 3 C. almond flour
- 2 C. rhubarb, chopped
- ½ tsp. salt
- 1 tsp. baking powder
- ½ tsp. cinnamon powder
- 1 Tbsp. butter, melted
- Cooking spray

Directions:

1. In a bowl, mix the milk with vanilla, lemon juice, and the other ingredients except for the cooking spray and stir well.
2. Pour into 2 loaf pans greased with cooking spray.
3. Bake at 350 degrees °F for 40 minutes, cool down, slice, and serve.

Nutrition/slice: calories 203, fat 4.7, fiber 2, carbs 4, protein 3.4

GINGER CANTALOUPE BREAD

Preparation Time: 10 minutes

Cooking Time: 1 hour

Servings: 2 loaves

Ingredients:

- 4 Tbsp. sugar
- 3 eggs, whisked
- 1 C. avocado oil
- 1 Tbsp. ginger, minced
- 1 and ½ C. cantaloupe puree
- 1 Tbsp. nutmeg, ground
- ½ tsp. almond extract
- 1 and ½ tsp. baking powder
- ½ C. ghee, melted
- 3 C. almond flour

Directions:

1. In a bowl, mix the flour with ginger, nutmeg, and all the other ingredients and stir really well.
2. Pour into 2 lined loaf pans and bake at 360 degrees °F for 1 hour.
3. Cool the bread down, slice, and serve.

Nutrition/slice: calories 211, fat 5.8, fiber 4.3, carbs 6, protein 3.8

APPLE BREAD

Preparation Time: 15 minutes

Cooking Time: 1 hour

Servings: 1 loaf

Ingredients:

- 1 C. brown sugar
- 2 C. white flour
- 2 tsp. baking soda
- 4 Tbsp. milk
- ½ C. butter, softened
- 1 tsp. almond extract
- 1 C. apples, cored and chopped
- 1 tsp. cinnamon powder
- 2 eggs
- 1 tsp. salt

Directions:

1. In a large bowl, mix the flour with the sugar, baking soda, and the other ingredients and stir well.
2. Pour this into a lined loaf pan and bake at 350 degrees °F for 1 hour.
3. Cool the bread down, slice, and serve.

Nutrition/ slice: calories 121, fat 3.2, fiber 2.3, carbs 5.4, protein 2

BANANA BREAD

Preparation Time: 15 minutes

Cooking Time: 1 hour and 10 minutes

Servings: 2 loaves

Ingredients:

- 2 bananas, peeled and chopped
- 2 C. white flour
- ½ C. melted butter
- ½ C. coconut oil, melted
- ½ C. almonds, chopped
- ½ tsp. baking powder
- ½ tsp. almond extract
- 1 C. sugar
- 2 eggs
- 1 tsp. baking soda

Directions:

1. In a bowl, mix the bananas with the flour, melted butter, and the other ingredients and stir really well.
2. Divide the mix into 2 lined pans and bake in the preheated oven at 325 degrees °F for 1 hour and 10 minutes.
3. Cool the bread down, slice, and serve.

Nutrition/ slice: calories 211, fat 4.3, fiber 3.2, carbs 6, protein 5.4

BLACKBERRY AVOCADO BREAD

Preparation Time: 10 minutes

Cooking Time: 50 minutes

Servings: 1 loaf

Ingredients:

- 2 C. white flour
- 2 avocados, peeled, pitted, and mashed
- 1 C. blackberries
- 1/3 C. honey
- 1 tsp. baking soda
- 1 tsp. baking powder
- 1 tsp. salt
- 1 tsp. nutmeg, ground
- 1 tsp. vanilla extract
- 2 eggs

Directions:

1. Take a bowl and mix the flour with the honey, baking soda, and the other ingredients and whisk well.
2. Pour into a loaf pan and bake at 350 degrees °F for 50 minutes.
3. Cool the bread down, slice, and serve.

Nutrition/ slice: calories 162, fat 4.3, fiber 3, carbs 5.1, protein 2.3

CHERRY BREAD

Preparation Time: 15 minutes

Cooking Time: 1 hour

Servings: 1 loaf

Ingredients:

- 2 C. cherries, pitted and chopped
- 2 C. white flour
- 1 C. sugar
- 2 eggs, whisked
- 2 tsp. baking soda
- ½ tsp. salt
- ½ C. coconut oil, melted
- ¼ C. cherry juice
- 1 tsp. almond extract
- 1 tsp. vanilla extract

Directions:

1. In a bowl, mix the cherries with flour, sugar, and the other ingredients and stir well.
2. Grease and flour a loaf pan and pour the batter into it.
3. Introduce in the oven at 350 degrees °F and bake for 1 hour.
4. Cool the bread down, slice, and serve.

Nutrition/ slice: calories 162, fat 4.5, fiber 4.3, carbs 12, protein 4.3

CHOCOLATE BREAD

Preparation Time: 15 minutes

Cooking Time: 1 hour

Servings: 2 loaves

Ingredients:

- 2 oz. dark chocolate, chopped
- 2 Tbsp. sugar
- 1 tsp. almond extract
- 3 C. almond flour
- 1 tsp. baking powder
- 1 tsp. salt
- ½ C. butter
- 2 eggs, whisked
- Zest of 1 orange, grated
- 4 Tbsp. orange juice
- 4 Tbsp. almond milk

Directions:

1. Heat up a small pan over medium heat, add the chocolate, sugar, and almond extract, and heat up for 2 minutes.
2. In a bowl, mix the flour with baking powder, chocolate, and the other ingredients and stir well.
3. Pour this into 2 small loaf pans and bake at 300 degrees °F for 1 hour.
4. Cool the bread down, slice, and serve.

Nutrition/ slice: calories 172, fat 4.3, fiber 3.4, carbs 7.6, protein 3.4

GINGER AND NUTMEG BREAD

Preparation Time: 10 minutes

Cooking Time: 40 minutes

Servings: 1 loaf

Ingredients:

- 1 tsp. sugar
- 1/3 C. warm water
- 1 tsp. active dry yeast
- 2 Tbsp. coconut oil, melted
- 1 C. milk
- 3 and ¼ C. all-purpose flour
- ¼ C. molasses
- 2 tsp. salt
- 2 Tbsp. ground ginger
- 2 Tbsp. butter, melted
- 1 C. brown sugar

Directions:

1. In a bowl, mix the sugar with the water, yeast, and the other ingredients, stir until you obtain a dough, and transfer to a working surface.
2. Knead the dough for 10 minutes, cover it, and leave aside to rise for 1 hour.
3. Transfer the dough to a loaf pan, cover the pan, and leave to rise for 1 more hour.
4. Introduce the pan in the oven at 350 degrees °F and bake for 40 minutes.
5. Cool down, slice, and serve.

Nutrition/ slice: calories 200, fat 1.4, fiber 2.3, carbs 5.4, protein 5.5

HONEY BREAD

Preparation Time: 10 minutes

Cooking Time: 50 minutes

Servings: 1 loaf

Ingredients:

- 3 cups all-purpose flour
- 1 tablespoon baking soda
- 1 teaspoon salt
- 1 teaspoon ground nutmeg
- 1/4 cup honey
- 1/4 cup maple syrup
- 1 cup beer (light beer or ale)
- 1/2 cup water
- 4 tablespoons melted coconut oil

Directions:

1. Preheat the oven to 350°F. Grease a 9x5-inch loaf pan or line it with parchment paper.

2. In a large bowl, whisk together the flour, baking soda, salt, and nutmeg.

3. In another bowl, mix together the honey, maple syrup, beer, water, and melted coconut oil.

4. Add the wet ingredients to the dry ingredients and mix until just combined.

5. Pour the batter into the prepared loaf pan and bake for 50-55 minutes or until a toothpick inserted into the center comes out clean.

6. Let the bread cool in the pan for 10 minutes, then transfer it to a wire rack to cool completely before slicing and serving.

Nutrition/ slice: calories 102, fat 3.4, fiber 4.5, carbs 7.4, protein 3.4

SWEET RED VELVET BREAD

Preparation Time: 20 minutes

Cooking Time: 50 minutes

Servings: 1 loaf

Ingredients:

- 3 eggs
- 1/3 C. vegetable oil
- ½ C. pumpkin flesh
- 1 box red velvet cake mix
- 1 Tbsp. sugar
- ½ C. milk

Directions:

1. Preheat the oven to 350°F and grease a 9x5-inch loaf pan.
2. In a large bowl, beat the eggs and vegetable oil together. Add the pumpkin puree and mix until well combined.
3. Add the red velvet cake mix, sugar, and milk to the bowl and mix until just combined. Do not overmix.
4. Pour the batter into the prepared loaf pan and smooth out the top with a spatula.
5. Bake for 50-55 minutes, or until a toothpick inserted into the center of the bread comes out clean.
6. Let the bread cool in the pan for 10 minutes, then transfer it to a wire rack to cool completely.
7. Once the bread is cool down, slice it and serve.

Nutrition/ slice: calories 152, fat 4.3, fiber 2.3, carbs 11, protein 3.2

VANILLA BREAD

Preparation Time: 15 minutes

Cooking Time: 1 hour

Servings: 1 loaf

Ingredients:

- 1 C. sugar
- 2 eggs, whisked
- 1/3 C. melted butter
- 2 tsp. vanilla extract
- 1 tsp. baking soda
- 1 tsp. nutmeg, ground
- 1 tsp. cinnamon powder, ground
- 1 tsp. salt
- ½ C. coconut milk
- ½ C. white flour
- 2 Tbsp. grated lemon zest

Directions:

1. In a bowl, mix the sugar with eggs and the other ingredients and whisk really well.
2. Pour this into a loaf pan and bake at 360 degrees °F for 1 hour.
3. Cool the bread down, slice, and serve.

Nutrition/slice: calories 162, fat 4.3, fiber 2.3, carbs 4.5, protein 2.3

TRIPLE CHOCOLATE BREAD

Preparation Time: 10 minutes

Cooking Time: 2 hours

Servings: 8

Ingredients:

- 1 C. of almond flour
- ½ C. of unsalted melted butter
- 1 ½ tsp. of flaxseed, ground
- 2 tsp. of unsweetened cocoa powder
- Keto sweetener Swerve, one tsp.
- Warm water, one C.
- Unsweetened almond milk, half a C.
- ½ tsp. of salt
- 1 tsp. of vanilla extract pure
- 3 eggs
- Active dry yeast, one and a half tsp.
- Baking powder, one tsp.

Directions:

1. Mix the eggs, pure vanilla extract, warm water, and almond milk.

2. In another mixing bowl, combine the almond flour, ground flaxseed, Swerve sweetener, salt, and baking powder.

3. As per the instructions on the manual of your machine, pour the ingredients into the bread pan, taking care to follow how to mix in the yeast.

4. Place the bread pan on the machine, and select the sweet bread setting, together with the crust type, if available, then press start once you have closed the lid of the machine.

5. When the bread is ready, using oven mitts, remove the bread pan from the machine. Use a stainless spatula to extract the bread from the pan and turn the pan upside down on a metallic rack where the bread will cool off before slicing it.

Nutrition: Calories 199, fat 8, fiber 2, carbs 13, protein 6

HONEY GRANOLA BREAD

Preparation Time: 10 minutes

Cooking Time: 2 hours

Servings: 13

Ingredients:

- 1 ¼ C. of unsweetened almond milk
- 2 tsp. of dry yeast that is active
- 3 tsp. of melted butter, unsalted
- 1 tsp. of cinnamon powder
- 2 ½ tsp. of honey
- Almond flour, three C.
- Salt, one and a quarter tsp.
- Granola, one C.

Directions:

1. As per your machine, pour the ingredients into the bread pan in the order prescribed by the manual; the machine needs to have a kneading paddle fitted into it.

2. Close the machine lid and select the basic bread setting on it. Press the loaf size and crust type buttons, as well, if they are available in the machine you are using. This is according to your desire.

3. Press start for the bread to begin mixing, kneading, rising, and, finally, baking.

4. When the bread is done, extract it, and place it on a metal mesh surface to cool before cutting it into desirable pieces.

Nutrition: Calories 240, fat 7, fiber 4, carbs 12, protein 12

APPLE BUTTER BREAD

Preparation Time: 10 minutes

Cooking Time: 2 hours

Servings: 9

Ingredients:

- Melted butter, half a C. unsalted
- Swerve sweetener, one C. An egg
- Unsweetened apple butter, one C.
- 1 tsp. of cinnamon powder
- Almond flour, two C.
- Baking soda, two tsp.
- Nutmeg ground, one tsp.
- Extract of vanilla, one tsp.
- ½ C. of unsweetened almond milk
- 2 tsp. of active dry yeast

Directions:

1. Mix the almond flour, Swerve, cinnamon, nutmeg powder, and baking soda in a container.

2. Get another container and combine the unsweetened apple butter, unsalted melted butter, vanilla essence, and almond milk that is unsweetened.

3. As per the instructions on the manual of your machine, pour the ingredients into the bread pan, taking care to follow how to mix in the yeast.

4. Place the bread pan in the machine and select the sweet bread setting, together with the crust type, if available, then press start once you have closed the lid of the machine.

5. When the bread is ready, using oven mitts, remove the bread pan from the machine. Use a stainless spatula to extract the bread from the pan and turn the pan upside down on a metallic rack where the bread will cool off before slicing it.

Nutrition: Calories 240, fat 7, fiber 4, carbs 12, protein 12

CINNAMON BREAD

Preparation Time: 10 minutes

Cooking Time: 2 hours

Servings: 9

Ingredients:

- Almond flour, one C.
- Baking powder, one tsp.
- Melted unsalted butter, three tsp.
- 4 eggs
- ½ C. of erythritol
- ¼ tsp. of tartar cream
- 1 tsp. of vanilla essence pure
- 2 tsp. of cinnamon powder
- ¼ C. of Swerve (sweetener)
- 1/3 C. of softened cream cheese
- 1 ½ tsp. of active dry yeast

Directions:

1. Combine in a mixing container the almond flour, sweetener, cinnamon, and baking powder.
2. Get a second container and add the unsalted butter, pure vanilla essence, eggs, tartar cream, erythritol, and softened cream cheese.
3. As per the instructions on the manual of your machine, pour the ingredients into the bread pan, taking care to follow the instructions in mixing in the yeast.
4. Place the bread pan in the machine, and select the sweet bread setting, together with the crust type, if available, then press start once you have closed the lid of the machine.
5. When the bread is ready, using oven mitts, remove the bread pan from the machine. Use a stainless spatula to extract the bread from the pan and turn the pan upside down on a metallic rack where the bread will cool off before slicing it.

Nutrition: Calories 211, fat 9, fiber 1, carbs 9, protein 3

CHOCOLATE BREAD

Preparation Time: 10 minutes,

Cooking Time: 2 hours,

Servings: 1

Ingredients:

- 1 pack active dry yeast
- ½ C. sugar
- 3 C. bread flour
- 1/4 C. cocoa powder
- 1 large egg
- 1/4 C. butter
- ½ tsp. vanilla extract
- 1 C. milk

Directions:

1. Mix ingredients and put everything in the pan of your bread machine.
2. Select the quick bread or equivalent setting.
3. Take out the pan when done and set aside for 10 minutes.

Nutrition: Calories 184, fat 5, fiber 2, carbs 12, protein 31

MIXED BERRY BREAD

Preparation Time: 10 minutes

Cooking Time: 3 hours

Servings: 5

Ingredients:

- 4 C. bread flour
- ¼ C. brown sugar
- 1/3 C. dried cherries, chopped
- 1/3 C. dried blueberries, chopped
- 2 tsp. yeast
- 1 ½ tsp. salt

Wet Ingredients:

- 1 C. water
- 2 Tbsp. vegetable oil

Directions:

1. After pouring the water and oil into the bread pan, add the dry ingredients to the mix.
2. Press the "Normal" or "Basic" mode of the bread machine.
3. Choose either a light or medium crust color setting.
4. Once the cycles are done, transfer the bread to a wire rack.
5. Cool down the bread completely before slicing.

Nutrition: Calories 145, fat 7, fiber 4, carbs 29, protein 4

GREEN TEA BREAD

Preparation Time: 1 hour and 10 minutes

Cooking Time: 1 hour

Servings: 1 loaf

Ingredients:

- 2 and ½ Tbsp. sugar
- 3 C. white flour
- 1 C. almond milk
- 2 eggs, whisked
- 1 Tbsp. green tea powder
- ¾ Tbsp. salt
- 2 Tbsp. butter softened
- 1 tsp. cocoa powder
- 1 tsp. vanilla extract
- 1 tsp. instant yeast

Directions:

1. In a bowl, mix the sugar with flour and the other ingredients except for the milk and stir.
2. Add the milk gradually, stir, and knead until you obtain a dough.
3. Cover the dough and leave it aside to rise for 1 hour.
4. Transfer to a loaf pan and bake at 375 degrees °F for 30 minutes.
5. Cool the bread down, slice, and serve.

Nutrition/ slice: calories 187, fat 3.4, fiber 2.3, carbs 12, protein 5.4

SOURDOUGH HERB CIABATTA

Preparation Time: 3 hours 10 minutes

Cooking Time: 30

Servings: 12

Ingredients:

- 1 Tbsp. of mixed chopped herbs
- 1 Tbsp. of salt
- 1 Tbsp. of olive oil
- ¾ C. of lukewarm milk
- 1 ¼ C. of lukewarm milk
- 1 C. of sourdough starter fed
- 6 C. of all-purpose flour

Directions:

1. Combine all the above ingredients in a stand mixer bowl
2. Use the dough hook to mix everything until an elastic, satiny, smooth dough is formed.
3. Grease a bowl, put the dough in it, and cover it with a tea towel. Leave it for 1 to 2 hours until the dough doubles in size.
4. Knead the dough out to deflate it.
5. Form the dough into a rectangle, and use a bench scraper to separate out 12 rolls.
6. Line a baking sheet using parchment paper and then dust it with flour.
7. Arrange the rolls onto a baking sheet and cover them using a kitchen towel for about 30 minutes.
8. Preheat oven to 425° °F.
9. Lightly dust the rolls with flour and then spray lightly with water.
10. Bake the rolls for 15 minutes.
11. Turn the baking sheet around and reduce the temperature to 375 °F. Then bake for 20 minutes more.
12. Once a deep golden crust has been formed, remove the rolls from the oven and leave them to cool down before serving.

Nutrition: Calories 388 Fat 12.8 g Carbohydrates 54.8 g Protein 17.3 g

SANDWICH SOURDOUGH BISCUITS

Preparation Time: 40 minutes

Cooking Time: 25

Servings: 8 biscuits

Ingredients:

- 1 C. of unfed sourdough starter
- 8 Tbsp. of cold unsalted butter
- ¾ tsp. of salt
- 2 tsp. of baking powder
- 1 C. of unbleached all-purpose flour

Directions:

1. Preheat the oven to 425 degrees Fahrenheit.
2. Place a rack on the oven's third top level.
3. Using parchment paper, line a baking sheet.
4. Mix the baking powder, flour, and salt in a mixing basin.
5. Mix in the butter with your hands to make a crumbly mixture.
6. Knead in the starting mix to make dough.
7. Flour your work area and pat the dough into a 1-inch thick circle.
8. Cut out 8 rounds with a biscuit cutter.
9. Place the biscuits on the baking pan and bake for 25 minutes or until golden brown.
10. Take the biscuits from the oven and set them aside to cool before serving.

Nutrition: Calories: 95 Fat: 7g Carbohydrates: 4g Protein: 1g

SOURDOUGH BREAD FOR SANDWICHES

Preparation Time: 5 hours 20 minutes

Cooking Time: 40

Servings: 1 loaf

Ingredients:

- 5 C. of flour bread
- 1 ½ C. of sourdough starter
- ½ a C. of warm water
- 2 tsp. of salt
- 2 Tbsp. of sugar
- 2 Tbsp. of butter
- ¾ C. of milk

Directions:

1. Mix the warm water, sugar, salt, and melted butter in a large mixing bowl. Combine the ingredients and stir.
2. Add the sourdough starter and mix until well combined.
3. Gradually add the flour to the mixture and mix until a sticky dough forms.
4. Knead the dough for about 10 minutes on a floured work surface until it becomes smooth and elastic.
5. Grease a bowl with some oil, place the dough inside, and roll it around to coat it with oil.
6. Cover the bowl with a clean kitchen towel and let the dough rise at room temperature for 2-3 hours or until it doubles in size.
7. Knead the dough for 3 minutes on a floured work surface.
8. Form the dough into a loaf shape.
9. Grease a baking sheet and place the dough on it for 45 minutes, covered with a tea towel.
10. Preheat the oven to 400 degrees Fahrenheit.
11. Slash a pattern over the top of the dough with a sharp knife.
12. Bake for 40 minutes or until the loaf turns golden brown.
13. Remove the bread from the oven and let it cool on a wire rack before slicing and serving

Nutrition: Calories 125, fat 5, fiber 4, carbs 12, protein 5

SOURDOUGH BOULE

Preparation Time: Overnight

Cooking Time: 1 hour

Servings: 1 loaf

Ingredients:

- 2 Tbsp. of extra virgin olive oil
- 1 tsp. of sea salt
- 2 Tbsp. of xanthan gum
- ½ a C. of rice flour
- ½ a C. of tapioca flour
- ½ a C. of buckwheat flour
- 1 ½ C. of millet flour
- 1 tsp. of apple cider vinegar
- 1 C. of non-dairy milk
- 1 C. of warm water
- 1 Tbsp. of coconut palm sugar
- 1 ½ C. of brown rice sourdough starter

Directions:

1. Whisk the nondairy milk and vinegar in a medium-sized mixing basin.
2. In a separate medium-sized mixing basin, thoroughly combine the sugar, start, and warm water.
3. Pour the milk-starter mixture into a mixing bowl and whisk to incorporate.
4. Add the flour and xanthan gum to the mixing bowl, kneading as you go.
5. Add the oil to the dough, then knead until it is evenly distributed.
6. Prepare a floured surface and oiled hands, then knead the dough.
7. With your hands, form a boule (round and flat) shape.
8. Line a bowl with parchment paper that has been dusted with flour.
9. Put the dough in the bowl, cover the bowl with a kitchen towel, and let it aside to rise overnight at room temperature.
10. Preheat the oven to 500 °F using a closed Dutch oven.
11. Using oven gloves, remove the Dutch oven from the oven and lay the dough seam side down into it. Bake for 30 minutes with the cover closed.
12. Reduce the heat to 450° °F and bake the bread for another 20 minutes.
13. Take it from the oven and put it on a cooling rack to cool fully before slicing.

Nutrition: Calories: 278; Fat: 2.9g; Carbs: 59g; Protein: 6.6g

SOURDOUGH WAFFLES

Preparation Time: overnight

Cooking Time: 20 minutes

Servings: 4 waffles

Ingredients:

- 2 Tbsp. of flax meal
- ¼ C. of vegetable oil
- ½ a tsp. of salt
- ½ a tsp. of baking soda
- 2 Tbsp. of sugar
- 2 tsp. of apple cider vinegar
- 2 C. of non-dairy milk
- 1 C. of buckwheat flour
- 1 C. of all-purpose flour
- 1 C. of brown rice sourdough starter

Directions:

1. Combine the vinegar and non-dairy milk in a medium-sized bowl.
2. In another medium-sized bowl, combine the sugar, flour, and starter, and stir together thoroughly.
3. Combine the milk mixture and the starter mixture and stir together thoroughly. Place a tea towel over the mixture and leave it to rise at room temperature overnight.
4. In the morning, combine the flax meal and 2 Tbsp. of water in a small bowl.
5. Add the oil, baking soda, and salt to the dough mixture, and whisk together to form a batter.
6. Heat the waffle maker and pour the batter into it.
7. Once the waffles become golden, remove them and serve.

Nutrition: Calories: 278; Fat: 2.9g; Carbs: 59g; Protein: 6.6g

SOURDOUGH PIZZA

Preparation Time: 1 day

Cooking Time: 35 minutes

Servings: 4

Ingredients:

- ½ a C. of arrowroot powder
- ½ a C. of sweet brown rice flour
- ½ a C. of brown rice flour
- 1 Tbsp. of extra virgin olive oil
- 1 tsp. of sea salt
- ½ a C. of filtered water
- ½ a C. of brown rice sourdough starter
- Pizza toppings of your choice

Directions:

1. Combine the water and starter in a medium-sized bowl and whisk together thoroughly.
2. Add oil and salt and whisk to combine.
3. Slowly add all the flour until you can begin kneading the dough.
4. Prepare a floured area and knead the dough for two min.
5. Grease a bowl and place the dough in it. Cover with a towel and let it sit for 24 hours at room temperature.
6. Prepare the oven by preheating it to 450° °F.
7. Grease a pizza pan with oil and spread the dough on it, don't use a rolling pin to press the dough out; use your hands.
8. Bake the dough until it begins to brown; this should take around 10 minutes.
9. Remove the dough from the oven and spread your toppings over it.
10. Bake again for another 20 minutes.
11. Once cooked, remove from the oven, slice, and serve.

Nutrition: Calories: 278; Fat: 2.9g; Carbs: 59g; Protein: 6.6g

BOOK 3

CHAPTER 8. EQUIPMENT NEEDED TO MAKE SOURDOUGH FROM SCRATCH

Equipment and Techniques

Consistency is one of the drawbacks of baking at home. It can be hard when the climate of our hectic home kitchens is continuously evolving. Here we have gathered all the tried-and-true methods in one place, and they will help you make your home kitchen bread simpler and more repetitive.

Sourdough baking does not require a lot of extra equipment, but the whole process will be made more accessible by other devices. Let's go over some favorite products for a moment and distinguish the "must-haves" from the "good to have."

Useful Tools

There are a few resources needed to bake your first loaf of bread. Despite the fact that this list may seem lengthy, your kitchen likely already contains many of the items on it — buy what you don't have.

First, it is to call your attention to a kitchen scale. Consider purchasing a cooking scale if you don't already have one. You can use it in your kitchen for so many things, and it pays for itself again and again. It is highly inaccurate to calculate flour with cups and scoops.

• Cooker hybrid, like a 3qt cabin cast iron combination cooker or le Creuset Dutch oven that can withstand 500 ° °F (260 ° c) in the oven and has a lid that can build a strong seal when sealed

- Two medium-sized kitchen bowls to prove the dough
- Bench knife to cut and shape
- Two kitchen towels or tea towels to line the bowls
- Kitchen scale weighing in grams
- Mixing bowl
- Instant-read thermometer
- White rice flour

After all those years of baking, sourdough starter continues to amaze everyone with its production, strength, and resilience every day. The use of glass jars to store your starter helps you to check on the operation of your starter. Additionally, they are a safe (i.e., non-reactive) and simple-to-clean medium.

Plastic dough scraper and stainless-steel bench knife: for effective handling of the dough, these two are a must. You can scoop the dough out of the bowl without deflating it too much with a plastic dough scraper and scrape the dough off your fingers (very useful when dealing with sticky flours such as rye or einkorn). Rinse it with water before using it to keep the dough from sticking to it.

A bench knife is more durable than a plastic scraper, and it is used to raise, shift, cut, and pre-form the dough. The handling of the bench knife is easy, requiring just a little practice; start using it, and you'll be handling dough like a ninja soon. After each use, wash them well, and store them until the next baking.

Digital scale: "freestyle" sourdough bread baking — that is, making the bread by feeling rather than precisely measuring the flour and water — can be fun to express yourself and very liberating. If you're looking for consistency in your baking, though, a digital electronic scale is worth your time. You can weigh everything that goes into your bread, from flour, water, and salt to starter sourdough and other add-ons.

We will be weighing our flour and water as we get our starter going. Measuring your ingredients before use makes the process easier; you will be sure of what you are pouring in and what you are taking out.

Pay attention to the following features when buying a digital scale:

- It should be lightweight
- Durable
- Easy to clean
- Able to carry a decent weight
- The number should be clear when the size of a large bowl is on.

Digital thermometer: this is for taking the temperature of our water and starter. It is essential to check the temperature of your water and starter just to be sure you are on the right track.

Three clear glass containers at least 24 oz. in size with a lid: you will need one container for your starter, one container for your discard, and one container to place your starter into when it is ready. I mentioned a clear container because you will need to keep an eye on your starter activity. Also, the cover does not need to be closed tightly; I would suggest you keep the top somewhat loose on your starter.

Apron: handling dough can be very messy from time to time, requiring your hands to be washed regularly (especially if you want to take pictures of your new baking creation too). If you're someone who thinks you can't find a dishtowel when you're most in need, an apron is a way out. One of the favorite kitchen accessories is cotton or linen aprons, as they make you feel decisive, fashionable, and like a smart, experienced housewife/husband. Additionally, resources may be placed in the front pockets of the apron.

Bread rising baskets (bannetons or brotforms): bread rising baskets are used to protect the soft dough as it rises; when you place them in the oven, they help the loaves maintain their shape and structure. You can experiment with various glass and plastic containers, and although improvising might be a great temporary solution, the container's material should enable the dough to breathe during its growth. Rising baskets can be used in different shapes (red, oval, rectangular) and materials such as cane, wicker, or wood fiber.

Sprinkle it with water and generously dust it with whole-grain flour before using the growing tub, or line it with a kitchen cloth (which you often dust with flour). This will allow the dough to roll away cleanly.

Baking stones or steels: recall the taste of a pizza cooked in a wood-fired oven; it would lead you to buy a granite baking stone. A baking stone's key advantage is that it mimics the effect of brick ovens by being able to uniformly control and retain a lot of heat, which is ideal for baking pizza and bread, as it helps to produce a deep, crunchy crust. To prevent thermal shock and fracturing of the baking stone or steel, a baking stone should be warmed and cooled along with the oven. Clay baking stones also cost less than granite ones.

Dough peel: a dough peel (aluminum or wood) will allow you to slide the dough onto the hot baking stone perfectly and easily, whether you are using it for pizza or bread. Make sure you sprinkle it with flour or cornmeal before placing a pizza on a peel to stop the dough from sticking. You may also place a piece of parchment paper underneath it when sliding bread onto a baking stone. After use, dust off or clean off your peel with a wet cloth.

Easy baking tins and trays: the sourdough bread with crispy crust could only be baked in a cast-iron Dutch oven; that's wrong. You can use baking tins and baking trays. You can choose between high-quality enamel vessels in various shapes and sizes and handmade ceramics. When properly cared for, they'll last a lifetime.

You can use tins for a baking sandwich and swirl bread and trays for cinnamon rolls and focaccias. In order to get a crunchy crust when baking in tins and trays, add steam by preheating another separate tray on the lower rack of your oven in the first minutes of baking. Throw some ice cubes or hot water onto the tray when loading into your bread. The water will evaporate, vaporize, and produce a crunchier layer.

Razor blades: inexpensive razor blades that can be bought at any beauty or hardware store are an effective device to score (slash) the bread before baking. By scoring the dough, making a signature bread decoration will spur your imagination. But most importantly, you can monitor how the dough expands in the oven, in which direction, and how much. In the oven, the expansion of the dough is also known as the spring of the oven. The depth and angle of the scores you make will produce different results and impact the magnitude of the oven spring as well.

If you find it too dangerous to keep the razor blade between your fingertips, mount it on a simple wooden handle (such as a coffee stirrer), or use some other scoring device, such as scissors or a very sharp knife. Scoring is the most beautiful when the dough has fermented to perfection.

Bread knife: a good slice is a regular, nice-looking, and untorn slice of sourdough bread. Investing in a serrated edge in a sharp bread knife is something you'll never regret buying. Your serving plate should look more elegant and delicate.

A Few Things to Note When Measuring:

Flour is considered the main ingredient in baking sourdough bread; the proportion of all the other ingredients to flour is called the percentage of the baker, and the water-to-flour ratio is regarded as the amount of hydration of the dough.

Mixing and Fermentation

The very first step in almost every sourdough bread recipe is to add ingredients to make the dough. But recipes seldom go into depth on how best ingredients can be combined. We will clarify methods for mixing the dough here to help you master the sourdough recipes.

The purpose of mixing dough is to blend dry and wet ingredients to create a sticky, tacky dough that will stay together on its own while being manipulated in various ways.

Although mixing dough is a relatively straightforward process, it can have a big impact on your finished product because it is your only real opportunity to make changes before baking your sourdough recipe. When a dough is formed, it is immune to changes in hydration and ingredient composition, so being vigilant about those variables is extremely necessary when the ingredients are first mixed.

Bread dough's simplest form contains only four main ingredients: water, flour, salt, and some kind of leavening agents such as commercial yeast or a natural sourdough starter. There is an endless range of flavoring possibilities beyond those four ingredients. For now, we'll concentrate on using a natural sourdough starter to blend bread dough. The following material is for general use and will refer to almost every sourdough recipe.

There are a few trade tricks that can really make a difference in your finished product when it comes to the technique for mixing good bread dough. Even the sequence in which the ingredients are brought to the bowl will affect the flavor and texture of the loaf. Although several methods are available for mixing dough, these step-by-step mixing instructions should place your dough in good shape to rise well and bake evenly. You will need your ingredients for this process, a large bowl (remember, the dough will expand!), measuring cups or a kitchen scale, clean hands, and a plastic spatula or scraper (optional).

- Measure water out. Be mindful of the temperature as it applies to your timetable. Remember, warmer water = proof for shortness, and cooler water = proofing for longer. Remove starter sourdough.
- Start by adding only one or so tablespoons of the starter: if it floats, your starter is ready to bake with it, and you can add the amount of starter your recipe recommends. You'll have to wait an hour or more to mix your dough, or your starter is just too young to use to bake. If it does not float in water, it will not be able to give the requisite rise to the bread.
- Break the starter up in the water using your hands to make a murky stream. This ensures an equal distribution of the starter in your bread dough.
- Add the flour and other ingredients but leave the salt out.

- Squish the ingredients together, wet and dry. Squeeze the wet and dry ingredients together with your hands or spatula until the flour is fully absorbed, and the dough just stays together-don't over-mix! Only add a little more water or flour, depending on how your dough feels at this point.

- Let the dough take 30-45 minutes to rest. Cover with foil or plastic wrap to avoid the development of a crust.

- Dissolve the salt in a bit of warm water and spill it over the surface of the dough. Squeeze your hands into the dough to force the salt down to the rim, and pinch the dough together to add the oil. Repeat until the salt feels absorbed, then give the dough a few folds in on itself so that the salt can be spread as uniformly as possible.

- Keep the dough soft, and either knead or no-knead.

Bulk fermentation (also known as the first rise or main fermentation) is one of the most important steps in baking leaven bread. When mixing ends, it begins right and lasts until the dough is separated and reshaped. The name means exactly what it is: a stage where the dough ferments in a huge, single mass. During this process, fermentation produces organic acids and gasses of carbon dioxide, both of which play an important part in the production of the dough. Organic acids are mainly what give the flavor and strength of the dough (acids help prepare the gluten network), and carbon dioxide provides consistency and lightness for the dough.

Although much of this research is performed by our friendly yeast and bacteria, the baker still profits from a regular check-in by the dough. Through a series of folds, we help to control dough temperature and strength, and such check-ins also give us a chance to decide how the dough is progressing.

Let the bulk fermentation proceed over 3 to 5 hours at room temperature for a standard sourdough bread recipe. Essentially, however, this period is determined by the bread you produce, what the ideal dough temperature reported is, and the temperature at which you hold the dough.

When to Avoid Fermentation in Bulk?

It takes practice to find the exact point when to stop bulk fermentation. You can learn to read the signs of adequate fermentation with time: dough strength, elasticity, smoothness, gain in volume, and bubbly appearance.

But it can be difficult to make the decision. Cutting bulk fermentation short may mean that your dough isn't fermented enough, and you're moving for an underproof result. If you move the bulk fermentation too far, on the other hand, the dough will be difficult to manage and on the verge of over-proofing. It's got to find a balance.

Look for a dough that has risen dramatically and is much smoother at the end of bulk fermentation than when bulk began. If you pull a little with a wet hand on the dough, you can feel both resistance and elasticity.

Look for life, also. Shake the bowl gently, and it'll jiggle, letting you know the dough has plenty of aeration. These are all fantastic signs the dough has fermented enough and is solid enough for the division.

Strong fermentation, adequate dough strength, finishing bulk fermentation at the right time, and complete proof – these are all steps needed for a beautiful bread loaf. And as you build a sense of how to deliver on each of these, with every bite, you can taste the difference.

Dividing and Shaping

There is a stage in the traditional life cycle of baking bread where the dough has to be shaped into its final shape. But right before that, there is a step that is often ignored but equally important: the pre-shaping of bread dough.

Pre-shaping is just as it sounds; it sets the stage for good final shaping — and a baker will take many approaches. Some people prefer firmly pulling the dough together and letting it rest with the seam facing up. Others gently pick the dough and make it rest seam-side-down on top for a perfectly smooth surface.

Ultimately, it's up to the baker to approach. Let's walk through some factors that can affect how your dough is pre-shaped.

What is it that Pre-Shaping Does?

Most bread recipes need enough dough to make several loaves, but slicing a large mass into perfectly shaped pieces can be difficult on the first attempt. Usually, you'll be left with lumps in different shapes and sizes.

Perform a pre-shape move to add some measure of uniformity to the parts to facilitate the final shaping of those unruly forms. This way, starting from a clear and organized structure, when we begin the final shaping of our dough — whether it's a boule, baguette, or something else.

Pre-shaping also gives us an extra opportunity to add some strength to our dough. When your split dough feels a little loose or slack, you can give it a tighter pre-shape. This simple act will add much-needed strength and stability to a dough, which may otherwise prove to be tricky.

Alternatively, if the dough is extremely thin, likely due to under-mixing or over-hydration, a second pre-shape step may be performed to add more structure to the dough before shaping. It guarantees a high rise in the dough and makes it less likely to fall or spread.

While pre-shaping is not strictly mandatory, it offers an opportunity for your dough to check in and assess its strength and fermentation activity. It sets the stage for a phase of becoming more streamlined.

Take a very gentle approach to reshape, as with other phases in baking; there is no best way to do something; it depends on your choice and how happy you are with it. It efficiently organizes and strengthens the dough without being too offensive. Now, though, it's important to make the call: is the dough a little on the weak side? If so, pre-shape it more strongly and in more order. Conversely, a very light hand will do if the dough is solid enough.

Think about how long you want to form the final shape after you've prefigured it. If the pre-shape-form interval is low, then gently pre-shape. If it is longer, then more assertively pre-shape.

Why Fold and Stretch?

Folding by a very basic sequence of acts helps to give energy to the bread dough: spread the dough out and over itself. This stretching and folding act, which only takes a few moments, helps the dough grow the gluten network. Every fold has a significant effect on the strength of the dough.

It also helps to control the dough temperature in the entire bulk mass. This means the temperature of the dough is fairly consistent throughout — no cold or warm spots at either the top or the bottom.

And finally, we have a chance to treat the dough at each package and get a first-hand evaluation of how it develops: is the dough slow because it is cool in the kitchen? This means that we might need to prolong the fermentation in bulk. Is it good enough for pre-forming, or requires another set of folds? We have a chance to answer those questions by interacting with the dough in this way and to change course as appropriate.

How Do I Fold In and Stretch?

This method works best when performing a series of fast folds and then letting the dough rest. If you attempt to execute another package too fast, you will find that the dough is too small. Stretching would be difficult and may even break. Consider spacing out each set by 30 minutes for most dough (with the first collection that occurs 30 minutes after bulk fermentation begins).

How to fold bread dough: there are several ways to fold bread dough, but it's your choice to do it in the bowl directly. Next, get a small water-filled cup, and place it next to your bulk container. To avoid unnecessary sticking, dip your hands in the water before folding.

A simple stretch and fold are performed with wet hands to prevent sticking.

Four times, you'll do the same up-and-over motion, turning the bowl after each fold. Use two wet hands and take the side of the dough farthest from you, then raise it and down to the side nearest to your neck. After that, rotate your container 180 °, wet your hands again if necessary, and do the same stretching and folding. Next, rotate the container 90 °. Take the side of the dough away from you; move it back and forth again to the side of the container nearest to your neck. Rotate your bowl to 180 ° and do the same fold one last time.

Gently pick the dough up in the middle to finish the package and let the ends fall just under a little bit. It helps keep the middle of the dough clean.

How Many Fold-Up Sets are Needed?

There is no single answer on how many sets you need for your dough. When mixing your dough by hand, it can be done in two to four pieces. Flour form and hydration in the recipe, of course, also play a major part in answering this issue. Generally speaking, the slacker the dough, the more folds we need to strengthen it fully.

There are also other types of dough that do not need to be folded for. For example, you should probably skip folding with 100 percent rye bread since the gluten properties in the rye do not reinforce wheat gluten in the same way. Also, if your dough is very rigid and has poor hydration — or if it has been mixed and kneaded before bulk fermentation to maximum growth — there is no need to impart additional strength via folding.

Final Proofing, Scoring, and Finishing

The final proof is a repetition of the fermentation of yeasts, which allows the relaxing and expanding of the molded dough portion. A piece of dough that has gone through the sheeting and molding process is degassed and lacks in length. Once baked, the final proofing produces an aerated dough of optimal shape and volume.

Proofing happens in a controlled environment of warm and humid conditions. In general, the proofing temperature is higher than the fermentation temperature at around 32–54 ° c (90–130 ° °F). In the final proof, three basic factors are important:

- Temperature - it is recommended a range of 35–37 ° c (95–100 ° °F). Temperature and time variables work closely together.
- Humidity – 85–95 percent relative humidity (rh). If humidity is too high, humidity condensation may occur on the dough, resulting in a tough crust and surface blistering in the finished bread. If the humidity is too low, dry skin on the dough may form, preventing expansion and causing discoloration of the crust.

- Time-the time for proofing will be 60–65 minutes—over proofing results in light crust-colored loaves, coarse grain, weak texture, and an acid overtone taste. Under-proofing produces limited loaf length, shell tops, insufficient flow, and bursting at the sides.

During the final proofing stage, enzymes transform the starch into sugars. Yeast thrives on sugars; it converts the sugars' carbohydrate source into carbon dioxide and alcohol when oxygen is not present. The dough rises because the carbon dioxide is stored within the cells that form in the protein matrix.

The final proof is essential for yeasted dough, which needs to regain its volume and elasticity after shaping so that it can be baked successfully. During the last proving stage, the yeast produces acids that contribute to the development of flavor. Inadequate proofing time can result in flat, dense bread since the dough's components haven't had enough time to relax and develop flavor.

The final proofing time varies with the type of dough being used. A maximum of 1 hour of proving time is required for dough made with a fast mixer. The high-quality, intensive-mix dough needs a final proving period of 1 to 2 hours. Bread leavened exclusively with sourdough starter requires additional time to proof.

The type of product, the amount of time the dough was mixed, the temperature it was baked at, the amount of fermentation it underwent, and the quality of the flour all play a role in determining the testing time and temperature. Sometimes the height of the loaf is used as a measure of when the dough has been sufficiently proven. During the proving phase, the dough will increase in volume by a factor of three or four. The dough's spring is another indicator that the proofing process is nearly complete. The dough is ready for baking when it can be gently pressed and bounces back to its original shape.

Pre-Shaping Steps for Bread Dough:

The aim of pre-shaping is to take each piece and form it into a loosely round form with just enough outside tension. The round will maintain its shape on the surface of the work but not be so tightly pre-shaped that the outer "head" begins to break. Avoid pre-forming when you find that the surface is smooth without creases and is fairly uniform all over — if you're too rough with pre-forming, you'll end up with a denser loaf of bread.

Turn the dough over a floured workboard. Then brush the dough with flour on top and break it into parts according to the desired weight of the dough.

Move the blade against the dough and roll it gently over the work surface as you move. Each of your hands works in unison: as you drive the blade into the dough, your empty hand tugs the dough under. The movement is swift and gentle; then, take your blade and hand out of the dough when it comes to rest on the workboard.

Repeat this motion with your blade and send it over and over, turning the dough gently every time. Through the move, you will find that the dough tightens further as it snags the surface of the dry work, and you hurry it along. This stretching on the outside of the dough will be noticeable as the skin stretches slightly and becomes taut.

Continue with these motions till the dough is in a loose, round shape. Neither clear seams nor bulging sides should be present. Start gently rounding the dough if there is, and smooth the top. The trick is finding the balance between just enough and not enough stress.

After all of your dough pieces have been pre-shaped, let them rest on the bench before shaping.

Until final shaping: bench rest. If you had to shape your dough immediately after pre-shaping, it would be too tight and could break. After giving the dough time to rest, you give it time to relax and spread in what's called the "bench rest." this gives the uniform pieces extensibility, allowing us to manipulate them into their final form.

Bench rest can usually range from 10 minutes to 45 minutes. The length depends on how solid your dough has been and how closely you have pruned it. The closer the pre-shape, the lengthier the bench can rest before relaxing enough.

Fast-cut the bench rest when you notice your dough spreads easily. Then, either take a second pre-shape step or continue straight away with the final shaping.

Conversely, if you stop shaping your dough, consider giving it more time to relax and rest.

Pre-shaping, as with most aspects of baking, requires time and special consideration. If you look closely, we can see how each movement brings order to pieces that once were shaggy parts. This paves the way for more effective shaping and greater consistency in baking.

What's the easiest way to get your pre-shape working? Find a recipe for bulletproof bread, double the ingredients, and perform. There is no substitute for building the confidence and intuition which comes with repeated training.

Importance of Environmental Condition

When you consider the kinds of baked goods found around the world, you will find that the regional environment influences their characteristics. Crusty bread, for instance, tends to come from more arid areas, while softer bread also comes from more humid regions. Given the access a bakery has to the finest available ingredients, it cannot import the environment from the country of origin of a nice. Climate management methods can be used to establish optimal conditions, however.

Storage: the need for sufficient levels of relative humidity begins in the storage room before the baking starts. If relative humidity levels are lower and temperatures are warmer, many ingredients perform their best and retain their consistency. Otherwise, the ingredients will decay faster as they oxidize, increase the weight of the water, and become susceptible to growth in the mold. Conversely, certain foods, such as fruit or icing, need higher relative humidity levels, or they will desiccate.

Also critical are the conditions under which you store and treat the baked goods, as temperatures and humidity levels influence the finished products and their shelf life. Excessively humid conditions soften crisp crusts, cause crackers to lose their crunch, or prevent the drying of dough, which is important for pasta. If the temperature control fails in the field, the products will quickly grow mold. Goods that customers consider to be soft and moist, such as cakes and sweet rolls, dry out excessively in arid conditions.

Although a bakery might be utilizing refrigeration and air-conditioning systems, condensation due to the moisture that freshly baked goods give off or condensation from oven exhaust might not be adequately prevented. Bakeries, therefore, benefit from the use of independent climate control technologies, which allow them to track and regulate the conditions in individual areas.

Dough proofing: the yeast is adaptive to its surroundings as a live organism. In flour, temperatures and relative humidity levels, the water content influences how it ferments. As proof of dough, yeast produces carbon dioxide, which causes the dough to rise, have a distinctive aroma, and change the gluten in it. Bakers also use dough fermentation rooms or proofing cabinets, or proofers to gain greater control over how yeast performs. Dough fermentation rooms need at least 75 percent of relative humidity. The relative humidity of the proofers is at least 80% to prevent skin from settling on the dough during the final stages of the proofing. Generally, the lower humidity makes the bread crustier as it bakes. Technologies for climate control integrated into the proofing areas maintain the temperature and humidity levels needed for the baked goods concerned. This is particularly beneficial during warm days when proofers appear to retain more heat.

Baked goods require more than putting the dough in the oven, as the quantity of water vapor in an oven influences baking times and the finished product. Forced convection ovens with lower temperatures have relative humidity levels of 30 to 60 percent. Natural convection ovens with higher temperatures have humidity levels of 90 to 95 percent. Baking times are longer when the humidity levels are higher, leading to the gradual evaporation of moisture and gluten coagulation in the crust. Arid conditions can cause over-baking and result in products that are too tough. The ideal type of oven and level of humidity to be used depends on the specific product being baked.

When your bakery conditions are of higher quality, you can produce higher yields, experience less food waste-related losses, and promote greater customer satisfaction.

Monitoring factors that affect the growth of microorganisms:

- Time: it will take several days of daily feeding to create a starter or rehydrate a dried starter. When ready to use, it will bubble and grow and produce a surprisingly sour scent.

- Temperature: the fermenting microorganisms are more viable at temperatures that are comfortable for you, at normal room temperature (around 70 ° °F). Fermentation slows at cooler temperatures, and when too hot for your comfort happens too fast or even ceases.

- Moisture: water mixed with flour provides the atmosphere required to grow wild yeast and bacteria. Hold the starter covered loosely to prevent the production of mold.

- Acidity: beneficial lactic acid bacteria (lab) produce lactic acid, which increases acidity and safely lowers the pH below 4.6. This rapid acidification of the sourdough starter will help limit the production, including mold, of harmful microorganisms.

- Nutrients: periodic periods of feeding are required. Removal of some starter for optimum microbial growth with each new introduction of flour and water assists with nutrient access. Flour type may also influence the production of the microbial and the final product.

- Oxygen: carbon dioxide is created by fermenting the sourdough starters. To release the gas safely, the starter should be loosely covered, but the culture does not require oxygen.

- Changes made to high altitude: remember that low humidity and low pressure at higher altitudes influence the preparation of the food.

CONCLUSION

Thank you for making it to the end of the book. As the world's population increases, so do the number of people interested in making sourdough bread. So, if you decide to carry on the centuries-old practice of baking this delicious and nutritious loaf, you won't be alone. What could start out as a few tentative, untested forays into the sourdough baking community for you can quickly become an integral part of your routine. Do not give up if your initial attempts to enlist the aid of wild yeasts and helpful lactobacillus bacteria are unsuccessful. You might interact with indigenous groups, and perhaps you can work together to everyone's benefit. You'll be able to make bread with incredible flavor, texture, and crunch thanks to the organisms you nurture, and they'll be able to thrive in your care. Sourdough bakers may treat their starter as they would a small pet, providing it with just enough love and attention to keep it alive. You won't again have to risk taking your beginning out for a stroll in the wet and cold again.

Happy baking!

Made in the USA
Las Vegas, NV
14 November 2023

80767441R00096